Colorado

BY THEME

DAY TRIPS

Aimee Heckel

Adventure Publications
Cambridge, Minnesota

Dedication

This book is dedicated to Betty Anne.

Acknowledgments

Thanks to my daughter, Betty Anne, and my husband, JD, for always being up for an adventure. There's no team I'd rather explore the world with.

Safety Note Colorado is home to a variety of potentially dangerous animals, including venomous snakes, scorpions, as well as natural hazards, such as temperature extremes, sudden flash floods, and cliffs and dropoffs. Always heed posted safety warnings, take common-sense safety precautions, and remain aware of your surroundings. You're responsible for your own safety.

Cover and book design by Jonathan Norberg
Front cover photo: Maroon Creek Valley and Maroon Bells (see page 73), Aspen, CO photo by **Sean Xu/ shutterstock.com**
Back cover photo: Cliff Palace ar Mesa Verde photo by **MarclSchauer/shutterstock.com**

All photos by **Aimee Heckel**, except pg. 120: **Danica Chang/shutterstock.com**; pg. 22: **Federico Cudrcio/ shutterstock.com**; pg. 94: **Sharon Day/shutterstock.com**; pg. 8: **Rich Flubacker/shutterstock.com**; pg. 126: **Arina P Habich/shutterstock.com**; pg. 17: **Hdc Photo/shutterstock.com**; pg. 78: **Jim Heckel**; pg. 93: **Tongra Janiaduang/shutterstock.com**; pg. 67: **laura.h/shutterstock.com**; pg. 49: **Mister Stock/shutterstock.com**; pg, 62: **pics721/shutterstock.com**; pg. 100: **Phillip Rubino/shutterstock.com**; pg. 12, 131: **Sopotnicki/shutterstock.com**; pg. 58: **STORM INSIDE PHOTOGRAPHY/shutterstock.com**; pg. 40: **The World in HDR/shutterstock.com**; pg. 87: **Traveller70/shutterstock.com**; pg. 57: **T.Schofield/shutterstock.com**; pg. 88: **Vern Underwood/shutterstock.com**; pg. 82: **US Department of the Interior_David Tarailo**; pg. 99: **Kris Wiktor/shutterstock.com**

These Flickr images are licensed under the Attribution-NoDervis 2.0 Generic (CC BY-ND 2.0) license, which is available here: https://creativecommons.org/licenses/by-nd/2.0/ - pg 50: **World Poker Tour**

These Flickr images are licensed under the Attribution 2.0 Generic (CC BY 2.0) license, which is available here: https://creativecommons.org/licenses/by/2.0/ - pg 105: **Heath Alseike**; pg 132: **jenniferlinneaphotography**; pg 137: **Mark Mauno**

10 9 8 7 6 5 4 3 2

Colorado Day Trips by Theme
Copyright © 2020 by Aimee Heckel
Published by Adventure Publications
An imprint of AdventureKEEN
310 Garfield Street South
Cambridge, Minnesota 55008
(800) 678-7006
www.adventurepublications.net
All rights reserved
Printed in China
ISBN 978-1-59193-891-0; ISBN 978-1-59193-892-7 (ebook)

Table of Contents

Great Sand Dunes National Park

COLORADO HAS MORE NATIONAL PARKS than almost
any other state. Rocky Mountain in the north is home to 124
named peaks; Great Sand Dunes in the south boasts the country's
tallest dune; Mesa Verde in the southwest is a step back in time;
and the western Black Canyon of the Gunnison is famous for its
steep gorge.

NATIONAL PARKS

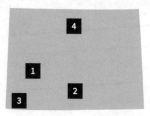

1 Black Canyon of the Gunnison National Park

South Rim Visitor Center: 9800 CO 347, Montrose; 970-641-2337, ext. 205
nps.gov/blca

Peek into the soul of the planet, as you peer into this dramatic, steep gorge, named for its unique black rocks. The Black Canyon presents some of the country's steepest cliffs and and some very old rocks, with some dating back 500 million years. Below, the Gunnison River promises outdoor adventure galore. Look for the famous Painted Wall, as well as wildlife, including deer, elk, and eagles. Gunnison is a bit farther of a trek from Denver and the bustling cities, so it tends to be one of the lesser-visited national parks. If you crave to be surrounded by nature with fewer crowds, Black Canyon of the Gunnison is well worth the drive.

2 Great Sand Dunes National Park & Preserve

Visitor Center: 11999 CO 150, Mosca; 719-378-6395
nps.gov/grsa

The highlight here is the tallest sand dunes in North America, which might come as a shock in a state not known for desert conditions. Coast down these dunes on special sand-boards and cool off in Medano Creek, which snakes through the preserve. Or just hike the dunes for a unique experience and excellent views. (Just make sure you pack plenty of water, because it can get toasty in summer, and there's not much shade.) It's a bucket-list item to conquer the tallest sand pile at 750 feet high, set to the backdrop of mountain peaks. Bonus: The sand dunes are open year-round, day and night, so you can go camping or even midnight hiking here.

3 Mesa Verde National Park

Mesa Verde Visitor and Research Center: 35853 Road H.5, Mancos; 970-529-4465
nps.gov/meve

Five thousand archaeological sites, including Ancestral Pueblo cliff dwellings, are preserved in this national park where ancient history comes to life. Mesa Verde boasts some of the best-preserved and most notable cliff dwellings in the country. Climb inside kivas, through tunnels, and up tall ladders, and experience what life might have felt like for Colorado's first residents. Mesa Verde is great for families; it's an educational vacation that is simultaneously active (prepare for lots of walking), scenic, and adventurous. There's a hotel and campground in the park, but if those are booked, you'll find cute cabins in the nearby mountains and hotels in the towns of Mancos and Durango.

4 Rocky Mountain National Park

1000 US 36, Estes Park; 970-586-1206
nps.gov/romo

Stand on top of it all in this national park, which boasts the highest continuous paved road in the country (Trail Ridge Road) and multiple peaks taller than 13,000 feet. A lifetime goal for many outdoor lovers, climbers, and fitness extremists (it's not an easy challenge) is to conquer Longs Peak. Rocky Mountain National Park is family-friendly and has offerings for all levels of ability. It is packed with outdoor adventure, including more than 350 miles of hiking trails, great wildlife-watching (such as bighorn sheep, elk, and eagles), plenty of fishing, and views that go on forever. Summer can get busy, so consider visiting in the fall, when the changing aspen leaves paint the forest a surreal gold. In winter, enjoy the park via sledding, showshoeing, or cross-country skiing. There aren't any ski resorts in the park.

Whitewater rafting on the Arkansas River

IF YOU'RE LOOKING for a heart-racing adventure out in nature, Colorado knows how to get that adrenaline surging. Find your fun up high on zip lines or low on a white-water raft in the base of a canyon. Test your strength on a steep trail, your courage on a high suspension bridge, your climbing skills on a frozen waterfall, and your mental limits in small, dark caves beneath the earth. These are just a few of the types of outdoor adventure you can fit into an action-packed Colorado vacation.

OUTDOOR ADVENTURES

1 Arkansas River *10*
Go whitewater rafting and fishing in these impressive, scenic waters.

2 Cave of the Winds Mountain Park *10*
Adventures await beneath the earth and above the canyon at this unique attraction.

3 Denver Adventures *10*
Enjoy Colorado from above when you try Colorado's longest and fastest zip line.

4 Manitou Incline *11*
Run or hike up this crazy-steep staircase in Colorado Springs, if you can make it.

5 Ouray Ice Park *11*
In the winter, climb a man-made ice wall in the mountain town of Ouray.

6 Royal Gorge Bridge & Park *11*
Walk across the highest suspension bridge in the nation to an adrenaline-filled amusement park.

7 Winter Park Resort's Alpine Slide *11*
After the snow melts, zoom down Colorado's biggest mountain slide, built on a ski slope.

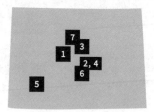

1 Arkansas River

Starts near Leadville and flows through Colorado

The Arkansas River, which starts near Leadville and flows through Colorado all the way to Arkansas, is a tributary of the Mississippi River and is the sixth-longest river in the nation. It's also one of the most popular white-water rafting destinations in the country, with more than 100 miles of rafting and a variety of difficulty levels, all the way up to Class V. For a calmer kind of rush, the Arkansas is one of Colorado's top fishing spots, with Gold Medal–rated waters. Fly-fish in Bighorn Sheep Canyon and explore the Upper Arkansas.

2 Cave of the Winds Mountain Park

100 Cave of the Winds Road, Manitou Springs; 719-685-5444
caveofthewinds.com

Explore dark, mysterious caves winding below Colorado Springs at the Cave of the Winds. These naturally occurring, underground caves transport visitors into a 4-million-year-old rock world, so deep that no light can penetrate. Sign up for different tours, including a ghost tour, if you're brave enough. Outside the caves, even more adventure awaits. Cruise across the canyon on a zip line or balance on an obstacle course on the edge of a 600-foot-high cliff. The truly brave hop on the Terror-Dactyl, a ride that shoots you into the canyon at almost 100 miles per hour.

3 Denver Adventures

26267 Conifer Road, Conifer; 303-984-6151
denveradventures.com

You'll find adventure outfitters throughout Colorado's mountains, but Denver Adventures offers the state's longest and fastest zip lines. Experience nature from above at speeds as fast as 60 miles per hour. These extreme zip lines stretch as long as 1,900 feet at up to 250 feet above the earth. After your ride (offered year-round, even in winter), you may want to add on a beer tasting: sip on up to eight different microbrews from across Colorado as you collect your nerves after the rush.

4 Manitou Incline

Starts at the Barr Trailhead, 7 Hydro St., Manitou Springs
manitouincline.com

This former cable car track has become an extreme hiking challenge in the Colorado Springs area. The hike is so steep that it covers more than 2,000 feet of altitude in just under a mile and can get as steep as nearly 70% grade. With 2,744 railroad-tie steps (way more than the Empire State Building), it's considered one of the highest sets of stairs on Earth.

5 Ouray Ice Park

280 County Road 361, Ouray; 970-325-4288
ourayicepark.com

This is Colorado's ice-climbing paradise. Every winter, the steep walls of Ouray's Uncompahgre Gorge are sprayed with water, which freezes to form jaw-dropping walls of ice that feature more than 100 ice and mixed climbs in 11 climbing areas. Adventure seekers come from around the world to scale these walls, but even if you don't have the skill or courage to climb yourself, the ice park makes stunning photos and captivating people-watching. It's otherworldly.

6 Royal Gorge Bridge & Park

4218 County Road 3A, Cañon City; 888-333-5597
royalgorgebridge.com

Here, you'll find a 10-mile-long canyon with steep, 1,000-foot cliffs. The Royal Gorge is known as the Grand Canyon of the Arkansas, referring to the river at its base. The Royal Gorge Bridge stretches across this breathtaking canyon; it's the highest suspension bridge in the country and was the world's highest until 2001. Yes, you can feel it sway, especially when the wind picks up. On the other side, you'll find more excitement, a carousel, playground, and Skycoaster ride among them. Take the scenic aerial gondola back and try to catch your breath.

7 Winter Park Resort's Alpine Slide

85 Parsenn Road, Winter Park; 970-726-1564
winterparkresort.com

In summer, this mountain is home to Colorado's longest alpine slide. Start by taking taking a chairlift up the Arrow Lift. Then hop on an alpine sled to fly, twist, and turn down a whopping 3,000 feet of track. The 600-vertical-foot plunge might sound intimidating, but you control the speed of your sled with an individual brake, and the track is smooth. Because you determine the speed, this ride is kid-friendly, though littler ones need to ride with a parent. This slide is typically open June–late September.

Cliff dwellings in Mesa Verde National Park

COLORADO BOASTS a rich Native American culture that existed long before European explorers arrived. From the famous cliff dwellings of Mesa Verde National Park to tribal parks to national monuments, you can easily center an entire Colorado vacation around Native American history. Take guided tours or self-guided explorations, like a journey through the vast Canyons of the Ancients National Monument. Some of the tribes that have roots in Colorado include the Anasazi, Arapaho, Cheyenne, Comanche, Jicarilla Apache, Kiowa, Pawnee, Shoshone, and Ute people.

NATIVE AMERICAN CULTURE

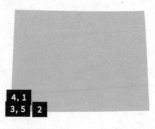

4, 1
3, 5   2

1 Canyons of the Ancients National Monument

27501 CO 184, Dolores; 970-882-5600
blm.gov/programs/national-conservation-lands/colorado/canyons-of-the-ancients

This national monument is a self-guided adventure hunt. Follow the map through 176,000 acres of open fields and on remote dirt roads to discover ancient sites and artifacts. The Canyons of the Ancients boasts more than 6,350 documented sites (plus tens of thousands more thought to be undocumented), giving it the highest-known density of archaeological sites in the nation. You'll witness kivas, rock art, old rock dwellings, petroglyphs, agricultural fields, sweat lodges, and shrines left behind from the former residents of this area. Nowhere else in the country can you find so many Native American artifacts in one place.

2 Chimney Rock National Monument

3179 CO 151, Chimney Rock; 970-883-5359
chimneyrockco.org

You'll know Chimney Rock when you drive past it. This sacred rock formation juts up out of the San Juan National Forest like a (you guessed it) chimney. It has deep importance in the history of the Pueblo residents who lived here more than 1,000 years ago, and you can learn all about it during a visit. See interesting artifacts and archaeological ruins, including about 200 homes and buildings, some of which you can explore. Hike to the top of the 7,000-foot-elevation site for panoramic views of the region. This site is a bit off the tourist path and tends to be less crowded than others in southwestern Colorado. You can also gaze at this site from the road as you drive past—it's hard to miss.

3 Hovenweep National Monument

Along the border between southeast Utah and southwest Colorado, just north and west of Cortez, Colorado (see website for directions); 970-562-4282, ext. 5
nps.gov/hove

Visit six prehistoric villages dating back to around the year 1200 at this national monument. Hike past ruins of impressive towers, pueblos, and cliff dwellings in Colorado's canyon country. Hovenweep used to be home to more than 2,500 ancient Pueblo people. The Square Tower Group loop is a highlight here and a great place to start. It contains the largest grouping of prehistoric structures. Immerse yourself in the culture and energy of the site by staying the night at Hovenweep's first-come, first-served campground.

4 Lowry Ruins National Historic Landmark

County Road 7.25, Pleasant View; 970-882-5600
blm.gov/visit/lowry-ruins-national-historic-landmark

The Lowry Pueblo monument is a highlight of the Canyons of the Ancients National Monument and a destination in and of itself. This impressive Ancestral Pueblo ruin contains 37 rooms; eight kivas; and one large, belowground kiva nearby. Walk through many of the rooms and down stairs beneath the structure to imagine how the Native American residents lived. The stone pueblo was built on top of abandoned pit houses around the year 1090. Historians believe as many as 50 people lived here at a time for about 165 years, until it was abandoned. It's considered one of the most important archaeological sites in the area.

5 Mesa Verde National Park

Mile 0.7, Headquarters Loop Road, Mesa Verde National Park; 970-529-4465
nps.gov/meve

Walk through history at Mesa Verde National Park, which features 600 Ancestral Pueblo cliff dwellings and almost 5,000 known archaeological sites. Dating back to the years 600–1300, Mesa Verde's dwellings are among the most famous and best preserved in the country. You can hike through many of the sites, including exciting options to scale tall ladders, explore cliffside above deep valleys, and scramble through tight tunnels. There's no park in the world quite like it.

6 Ute Mountain Ute Tribal Park

Junction of US 160 and US 491, Towaoc; 970-565-9653
utemountaintribalpark.info

Learn about the Ute Mountain Ute tribe and its history through ancient pictographs, petroglyphs, geological land formations, and historical sites in this tribal park. The artifacts here are preserved in their original state, and you can access them only with a Ute guide; no self-guided tours allowed. You can even go camping or rent a cabin on this sacred land to fully immerse yourself in Native American culture and energy.

7 Yucca House National Monument

Off County Road 20.5, Cortez; 970-529-4465
nps.gov/yuho

If you want to see Ancestral Pueblo life largely untouched by modern society, head to the Yucca House. This national monument has not been excavated, so it presents one of southwestern Colorado's biggest archaeological sites as its residents left it about 800 years ago. The Yucca House has two main areas: The West Complex is estimated to contain 600 rooms, 100 kivas, and a great kiva. The Lower House is smaller, with eight rooms and one kiva. All of the ruins are covered in vegetation, and a spring runs through the Western Complex. There's a feeling of discovery here, like you're the first explorer to stumble upon something remarkable.

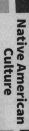

Chimney Rock National Monument

Garden of the Gods

YOU COULD NEVER NARROW DOWN the best spots to
visit on a nature-centric vacation in Colorado; there's just too
much natural beauty. But here are a few of our favorites, from
the widely popular and famous spots, like the surreal Garden
of the Gods and the scenic San Juan National Forest, to some
lesser-known gems. The Paint Mines park, with its strangely dyed
rocks; a peaceful, artistic sanctuary in Aspen; and the world's
highest botanic garden are a few outdoor destinations you may
not know about. As a bonus, all of these spots are accessible to
people of all ages and physical abilities.

NATURE

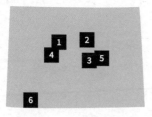

1 Betty Ford Alpine Gardens

183 Gore Creek Drive, Vail; 970-479-7365
bettyfordalpinegardens.org

While the mountain town of Vail is most famous for its ski slopes in the winter, a lesser-known gem is its internationally acclaimed gardens, featuring a unique spread of mountain plants from around the world. The Betty Ford gardens are the world's highest botanic gardens, located at 8,200 feet above sea level. At the Education Center, visitors can learn about alpine plant life via interactive and self-guided activities. The gardens draw more than 100,000 visitors every year. The site is named after former president Gerald Ford's wife, who lived in Vail Valley and enjoyed gardening and flowers.

2 Denver Botanic Gardens

1007 York St., Denver; 720-865-3500
botanicgardens.org

Immerse yourself in nature right in Denver at the Botanic Gardens. This 24-acre public garden encompasses a tropical conservatory, an amphitheater, and multiple gardens: gardens of the West (arid gardens showcasing Colorado native plants); gardens inspired by Japan, China, South Africa, and the Tropics; ornamental gardens packed with color and annuals; bird-filled shade gardens great to visit on hot days; and water gardens bursting with aquatic plants. Stroll through the gardens, enjoy summer concerts, and attend special events, like a corn maze in the fall, which takes place at Chatfield Farms, the gardens' 700-acre native plant refuge and farm in Littleton.

3 Garden of the Gods

1805 N. 30th St., Colorado Springs; 719-634-6666
gardenofgods.com

Giant red-rock formations jut up from the ground, while others stack on each other and balance in ways that seem to defy gravity. The Garden of the Gods is surreal and one of Colorado's most visited natural attractions. This National Natural Landmark was formed millions of years ago along a fault line, during the creation of the Rocky Mountains. Ancient Native American artifacts have been found here, indicating people have been drawn to the rocks for ages. Today, one of the best ways to explore it is by hiking along the 15 miles of trails. Experienced climbers also take to the sides of the vertical rocks for a challenge. This free park in Colorado Springs is open year-round.

4 John Denver Sanctuary

470 Rio Grande Place, Aspen; 970-920-5120
aspenrecreation.com/parks/john-denver-sanctuary
aspenchamber.org/explore-aspen/trip-highlights/john-denver-sanctuary

There are so many scenic places to visit in the Colorado outdoors, and so many in the mountain town of Aspen, too. But the John Denver Sanctuary is a lesser-known gem that's perfect for an afternoon stroll and picnic on the Roaring Fork River. This scenic, winding, waterside garden was built in memory of internationally famous musician John Denver. In fact, this isn't far from where he wrote "Rocky Mountain High." As you wander through the rocks, wetlands, trickling streams, and largest perennial flower garden in Aspen, you will encounter song lyrics etched onto rocks. The artistic rocks form a circle, representing the circle of life.

5 Paint Mines Interpretive Park

29950 Paint Mines Road, Calhan; 719-520-7529
communityservices.elpasoco.com/parks-and-recreation/paint-mines-interpretive-park

You have to see this park to believe it's real. In Calhan, rock formations look like someone painted them a rainbow of colors. Bands of colorful stripes, created by oxidized iron compounds, line the clay rocks. The colors have been drawing people for ages. In fact, historians have dated artifacts here back 9,000 years, and American Indians once used the naturally colorful clay to make paint—hence the name of the park. Beyond taking photos and gawking, you can go hiking in this 750-acre park, including a 4-mile loop trail with interpretive signs where you can learn about the history of the area.

6 San Juan National Forest

15 Burnett Court, Durango; 970-247-4874
fs.usda.gov/sanjuan

Colorado has 11 national forests spanning millions of acres, and they're all interesting for different reasons. While it's hard to narrow it down to just one, San Juan National Forest stands out for several reasons. First, it offers all kinds of outdoor exploration, from hiking to camping. But its scenic drives also make it highly accessible for people with kids, physical limitations, or limited time. In addition, this forest contains some of Colorado's richest history, from ancient Pueblo ruins to old mining towns with abandoned mills. Nature is diverse here, too, from mountaintops to desert mesas. The forest spans 1.8 million acres in southwest Colorado.

Red Rocks Amphitheatre

IMMERSE YOURSELF in Colorado art, and prepare to be amazed. Colorado takes advantage of its natural beauty by bringing the creativity outdoors. Watch Shakespeare performed under the night sky, stroll through art districts, and see a concert in the world's only naturally occurring, acoustically perfect outdoor amphitheater, Red Rocks. See local and national stars at annual events like the Cherry Creek Arts Festival and the Vail Dance Festival. Or make art the center of your vacation when you stay in the Golden Triangle Creative District, an inspiring stretch of Denver where art is everywhere, indoors and out.

THE ARTS

```
     ┌───┐
     │ 3 │
┌────┴───┴┐
│1, 2, 4-6│
└─────────┘
```

1 Central City Opera

Box office: 124 Eureka St., Central City; 303-292-6700
centralcityopera.org

See world-renowned performances set in a picturesque mountain backdrop at the Central City Opera. This opera has been wowing audiences since 1932, making it the fifth-oldest professional opera company in the nation. Since then, it has earned international acclaim and draws incredible performers to its 550-seat opera house built in 1878. Bonus: It's a short drive from Denver, and Central City is a hoppin' casino town sprinkled with Victorian buildings. It's totally worth making a weekend getaway, or longer.

2 Cherry Creek Arts Festival

Second and Third Avenues from Clayton Street to Steele Street, Denver; 303-355-2787
cherrycreekartsfestival.org

The Cherry Creek Arts Festival has been included among the nation's best outdoor arts festivals time and time again. It's a free weekend of world-class visual, performance, and culinary art that draws about 330,000 attendees. At the event, you can interact with hundreds of internationally respected artists, catch live music and performances on multiple stages, watch art being made, enjoy interactive exhibits, and eat high-quality food. The award-winning arts festival is run by a nonprofit that aims to support the arts throughout Colorado. The event started in 1991 and has become one of Denver's most exciting arts events. Attend it in the first weekend of July.

3 Colorado Shakespeare Festival

CU Presents: 972 Broadway, Boulder; 303-492-8008
cupresents.org/series/shakespeare-festival

Watch Shakespeare's classics performed under an open night sky at the Colorado Shakespeare Festival, put on by CU Presents. Every June in Boulder for more than 60 seasons, the beautiful Mary Rippon Outdoor Theatre has brought professional actors to the stage. You can also catch the shows indoors at the University Theatre on the

University of Colorado Boulder campus. Before some shows, enjoy informational talks about the play and stroll through the Colorado Shakespeare Gardens, filled with plants referenced in Shakespeare's plays. After the show, you can typically attend talkbacks with the actors.

4 Denver Performing Arts Complex

1400 Curtis St., Denver; 720-865-4220
artscomplex.com

Visit one of the country's largest performing arts centers, where you can see Broadway tours and Tony-winning shows, as well as some of Colorado's best performances. The center seats more than 10,000 in total and has 10 performance spaces, including the Ellie Caulkins Opera House, one of only three opera houses in the country with seatback tilting for every seat. It's the home base for many of Colorado's most prestigious performance groups, including the Colorado Ballet, the Colorado Symphony, Opera Colorado, and the Denver Center Theatre Company. You can also take acting classes, if you want to be the star yourself.

5 Golden Triangle Creative District

Area bounded by Speer Boulevard, Broadway, and Colfax Avenue, Denver; 720-828-0163
goldentriangleofdenver.com

In this one area of Denver, you can visit more than 15 galleries and museums, see public art, walk through scenic Civic Center Park, and more. The Triangle spans 45 city blocks between Speer Boulevard, Colfax Avenue, and Lincoln Street. Highlights include the Denver Art Museum, the Clyfford Still Museum, the Kirkland Museum of Fine & Decorative Art, and the Art Hotel, a hotel blended with an impressive art gallery where famous works may be in your room. A fun way to experience the Golden Triangle is on Final Fridays, the last Friday of every month, when creative businesses open their doors to the public.

6 First Friday Art Walks in the Art District on Santa Fe

Along Santa Fe Drive from 13th Street to Alameda Avenue, Denver; 720-773-2373
denversartdistrict.org/first-friday

The Art District on Santa Fe is a nationally respected art district filled with hundreds of galleries, theaters, restaurants, and more. A highlight here is the First Friday Art Walks, held (you guessed it) on the first Friday of the month year-round. These events draw thousands of visitors who come to stroll through the streets, pop into galleries, meet artists, watch art being made, and socialize. In fact, the area

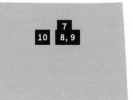

boasts the highest density of art galleries in the country. Local tip: If your feet get sore, hop on the free shuttle that circles the district every 20 minutes. The Art District on Santa Fe, a nonprofit, was named one of Colorado's first Certified Creative Districts.

7 Frequent Flyers Aerial Dance

3022 E. Sterling Circle, #150, Boulder; 303-245-8272
frequentflyers.org

If you like Cirque du Soleil and innovative dance—in the air—you will love Frequent Flyers. This aerial dance studio and performance company is one of the best in the world, and its annual Aerial Dance Festival draws dancers and teachers from all around. It was Colorado's first aerial dance school and offered the first professional program to train dancers in aerial dance, and its founder co-authored the first book on the topic. Lots of firsts here. If you want to learn how to fly high or low, this school can teach you. Or if you'd prefer to watch in awe from the crowd, the company puts on regular performances.

8 Museum of Contemporary Art Denver

1485 Delgany St., Denver; 303-298-7554
mcadenver.org

This museum opened in 1996 as Denver's first dedicated home for contemporary art, and it continues to explore that through rotating exhibitions and programs. There's no permanent collection here, which means every visit to the museum feels new; exhibitions switch out every few months. The museum features artists from local names to international innovators and has showcased the likes of Tatiana Blass, Jonas Burgert, and Dana Schutz, to name a few. After browsing the art, head to the rooftop deck and café to enjoy views of downtown Denver.

9 Red Rocks Amphitheatre

18300 W. Alameda Pkwy., Morrison; 720-865-2494
redrocksonline.com

This has to be the most interesting concert venue, set amid dramatic red rocks that create the world's only naturally occurring, acoustically perfect amphitheater. By night, listen to some of the world's top musicians under an open sky, with views overlooking the metro area. By day, the venue is used for tons of other purposes: fitness classes, yoga, hiking, history tours, and more. Watch classic films, grab a bite to eat, and explore the trails through the surrounding 738 acres. Historians think Red Rocks was used by the Ute tribe before its modern incarnation.

10 Vail Dance Festival

Gerald R. Ford Amphitheater (main box office): 530 S. Frontage Road E., Vail; 970-845-8497
vaildance.org

The Vail Dance Festival is considered one of the world's top summer dance events. For 30 years, this two-week festival has put Vail on the dance map, beginning with the 1989 performances of Moscow's Bolshoi Academy, which marked the first time the prestigious academy had toured the United States in 40 years. After that, the academy decided to make Vail home to its sole North American satellite school. Over the years, this cultural exchange evolved to become the annual festival that it is today, drawing dancers and spectators to celebrate world-class dance. It is typically held late July through early August and brings some of the world's best dancers to Vail Valley.

The Arts

Cheyenne Mountain Zoo

IF YOU WANT TO PLAN an educational and fun vacation around museums and animals, Colorado has some places you can't experience anywhere else. For an excursion right in the city, the Denver Zoo is home to more than 600 species, or if you prefer to see animals running free, there's The Wild Animal Sanctuary in Keenesburg. For underwater life, Denver's Downtown Aquarium is a must-visit, and for creepy-crawlies and winged critters galore, Colorado has the unique Butterfly Pavilion. As for museums, take your pick based on what you're into: art, nature and science, history, and more. Denver even has a special museum just for kids.

MUSEUMS AND ZOOS

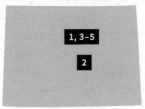

1 Butterfly Pavilion

6252 W. 104th Ave., Westminster; 303-469-5441
butterflies.org

Butterflies aren't the only critters you will experience at this unique, indoor tropical paradise, although the hundreds of fluttering butterflies are a highlight. In the Wings of the Tropics exhibit, stroll through a 7,200-square-foot man-made rainforest environment while free-flying butterflies dive and soar around your head. This climate-controlled conservatory also houses more than 200 types of plants from around the world. At the Butterfly Pavilion, you can also see a wide range of insects, underwater invertebrates, spiders, and more. Feeling brave? You can hold Rosie the tarantula. Want to get your hands dirty? Dig through soil and play with beetle grubs. The Butterfly Pavilion opened in 1995 as the first stand-alone, nonprofit insect zoo in the country.

2 Cheyenne Mountain Zoo

4250 Cheyenne Mountain Zoo Road, Colorado Springs; 719-633-9925
cmzoo.org

Visit one of the best zoos in America, where you can hand-feed giraffes lettuce and experience more than 750 animals, including more than 30 endangered species. This is the country's only mountainside zoo, built on the side of the peak at 6,714 feet elevation. It's not every day you can see Australian wallabies, gaze at elephants, and hand-feed cockatiels on the side of a mountain in Colorado Springs. The zoo also works to help protect endangered species and raise money for conservation efforts. One of the most unique exhibits here is the Scutes Family Gallery, which looks like a modern art gallery, except the sculptures are home to living snakes.

3 Children's Museum of Denver

2121 Children's Museum Drive, Denver; 303-433-7444
mychildsmuseum.org

The Children's Museum of Denver is filled with hands-on, interactive exhibits for kids to learn from and play with. Designed for kids age 8 and younger, activities center around exploring, creating, and investigating. Kids can play firefighter in a pretend fire station; visit a mini grocery store; read in a cozy Book Nook; learn about science via bubbles, water, and kinetics; and get crafty in the art studio. The list of fun spans about 20 exhibits. The nonprofit museum sees more than half a million visitors every year. Fun fact: It started as a converted school bus in the 1970s and has grown to cover a 9-acre campus. Set aside 1–3 hours for your visit.

4 Denver Art Museum

100 W. 14th Avenue Pkwy., Denver; 720-913-0130
denverartmuseum.org

The Denver Art Museum is an art lover's must-see because it's one of the largest art museums between Chicago and the West Coast. The museum is famous for its incredible American Indian art collection (closed at press time during renovations to the Martin Building, scheduled to be completed in summer 2020). In total, visitors can see more than 70,000 pieces from around the world in 12 permanent exhibits—everything from Asian to African, textiles to photography. The museum started in the late 1800s and has had a variety of homes and shapes, including an addition in 2006 that's a work of art in and of itself. The current complex spans more than 350,000 square feet and is a well-known Denver landmark.

5 Denver Museum of Nature & Science

2001 Colorado Blvd., Denver; 303-370-6000
dmns.org

See dinosaur bones, ancient fossils, outer space discoveries, Egyptian mummies, and more right in Denver. This family-friendly museum has been one of Colorado's top attractions for more than 100 years. Exhibitions and Imax films change regularly, so the museum is alive and always evolving. You may learn about nature, gemstones, or the human body. Highlights include the remnants of a triceratops found in nearby Thornton and fossils of Ice Age animals recently uncovered in a Colorado ski area. Many exhibitions are interactive, with creative challenges, puzzles, or brainteasers. On chilly days, the planetarium is a great way to warm up.

9
6, 7, 8, 10

6 Denver Zoo

2300 Steele St., Denver; 720-337-1400
denverzoo.org

This is the most popular paid place to visit in the Denver area, and for good reason. Arranged in a loop over more than 80 acres, the Denver Zoo houses 550 species, from rhinos to elephants to polar bears, and offers up-close encounters with many of the animals, including sea lions, giraffes, flamingos, penguins, and elephants. In 2020, a new animal hospital with a viewing area will allow guests to watch veterinarians working with the animals. The zoo holds special events throughout the year, like Boo at the Zoo in October and holiday lights in the winter. Conservation and education are also an important part of the facility. The Denver Zoo began in 1896 when a black bear cub began living at City Park and is now on the National Register of Historic Places.

7 Downtown Aquarium

700 Water St., Denver; 303-561-4450
aquariumrestaurants.com/downtownaquariumdenver

Hang out with mermaids, stingrays, and glowing jellyfish at the Downtown Aquarium in Denver. This massive aquarium is home to more than 500 species organized in varied habitats, from coral reefs to the desert. See Colorado native fish; saltwater fish from around the globe; and five species of sharks in the Shark Cage Experience, where you can dive into a 400,000-gallon shipwreck scene and encounter sharks from an underwater cage. Too scary? You can also watch a mermaid show. After exploring under the sea, head to the restaurant and lounge, where you dine in view of the fish.

8 Molly Brown House Museum

1340 Pennsylvania St., Denver; 303-832-4092
mollybrown.org

You've heard of "The Unsinkable Molly Brown." Now you can visit her former home. The Molly Brown House Museum was the residence of Margaret "Molly" Brown, who survived the RMS *Titanic,* the infamous ship that sank in 1912. Her Victorian house was saved from demolition and transformed into a museum in the 1970s, and today it draws about 45,000 visitors a year. Walk through the Queen Anne–style architecture and learn about Brown, the *Titanic,* and Denver's history. Look for special events, too, like tea parties and ghost tours around Halloween. Brown died in 1932, during the Great Depression.

9 The Wild Animal Sanctuary

2999 County Road 53, Keenesburg; 303-536-0118
wildanimalsanctuary.org

This is not a zoo, but you can see more than 460 lions, tigers, bears, leopards, wolves, mountain lions, and smaller carnivores, such as lynx and foxes. You may also see horses, emus, camels, ostriches, and more. The Wild Animal Sanctuary rescues animals from abusive or illegal situations and provides wide-open habitats for them to thrive. Don't expect cages and showtimes here. Instead, stroll along an elevated, 1.5-mile walkway and try to spot the animals roaming freely. The sanctuary is not about entertainment but about rescuing and providing homes for abandoned and neglected animals. It runs two sites in Colorado spanning more than 10,000 acres total. Plan 3–6 hours to visit this special site.

10 Wings Over the Rockies Air & Space Museum

7711 E. Academy Blvd., Denver; 303-360-5360
wingsmuseum.org

See more than 50 iconic aircraft and spacecraft, try out realistic flight simulators, check out historical military uniforms, and learn more about the US Air Force. Wings Over the Rockies is set up in the hangar of the former Lowry Air Force Base. Learn all about the history of the base through artifacts, archives, and a library, or arrange for your child to attend one of the regular special events, such as its Wings Aerospace Pathways, especially for middle school and high school students. This museum draws about 160,000 visitors from around the world every year.

Pagosa

WHEN MANY PEOPLE PLAN a vacation to Colorado, they think about ski resorts. But there's another way to experience Colorado's mountains, and it's all warm and bubbly. Colorado is home to naturally occurring, hot mineral water that bubbles up to form pools. You can find some in the heart of nature and others in spas and recreation centers. Some are located near the ski slope, so you can warm up your chilly toes after a day shredding the powder.

HOT SPRINGS

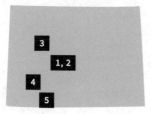

1 Chaffee County

Cottonwood Hot Springs Inn & Spa: 18999 County Road 306, Buena Vista;
719-395-6434
cottonwood-hot-springs.com/colorado
Mount Princeton Hot Springs: 15870 County Road 162, Nathrop; 719-395-2447, ext. 0
mtprinceton.com

Chaffee County, on the scenic Continental Divide, is known for having more fourteeners (mountains 14,000 feet high or higher) than anywhere else in the state, and it's also known for great hot springs. Stay at the Cottonwood Hot Springs Inn & Spa, a casual, off-the-grid motel near Buena Vista, and relax in multiple private geothermal mineral pools right outside your door. Nearby, you'll also find Mount Princeton Hot Springs in Nathrop, featuring three cascading Japanese-style pools; a 105°F soaking pool; an adults-only pool; a water slide and lazy river; a spa; and more. Stay in a cabin or hotel room, and cool off in the creek that runs through the property. Other area hot spots include the Hot Springs Aquatic Center in Salida and the Alpine Hot Springs Hideaway, Antero Hot Springs Cabins, and Creekside Hot Springs Cabin, all in Nathrop.

2 Colorado Historic Hot Springs Loop

colorado.com/hotspringsloop

Toasty, mineral-rich thermal waters naturally bubble up in western Colorado to make hot springs. Plan an entire trip around these pools by following the Hot Springs Loop. This one- to two-week road trip takes you to five spots in western Colorado: Chaffee County, Ouray County, Pagosa Springs, Glenwood Springs, and Steamboat Springs. (That's the ideal order to visit them in.) The total loop spans about 720 miles, but it's only a few hours in the car between the stops if you hit only one location per day (or longer), so you have plenty of time for relaxing. The 19 featured destinations all have multiple hot springs, and each spot is unique: some are in the heart of nature; others are family-friendly with water slides; and there are even adult-only, clothing-optional springs on this loop.

3 Glenwood Springs

Glenwood Springs Visitor Center: 802 Grand Ave., Glenwood Springs; 970-945-6580
visitglenwood.com

Glenwood Springs, set in the Rocky Mountains and surrounded by the White River National Forest, is famous for its hot springs, in particular the Glenwood Hot Springs, which claims to be the world's largest mineral hot springs pool. This popular pool looks like a regular, extralong, outdoor swimming pool (with lovely mountain views), except the water temps hover around 90°F–93°F. If Glenwood Hot Springs is too busy for you, check out Iron Mountain Hot Springs, a modern, quieter spot on the bank of the Colorado River, with 16 geothermal pools and a cooler family pool. Also worth visiting: the Yampah Vapor Caves, which are steamy, dark, peaceful, and underground.

4 Ouray County

Ouray Visitors Center: 1230 Main St., Ouray; 970-325-4746
ouraycolorado.com/hot-springs

Ouray's nickname is the "Switzerland of America" for its mountain views—it's surrounded by stunning mountains on all sides. Tucked inside Ouray County you will find five sulfur-free hot springs (meaning no stinky egg smell). You can stay where you soak at Box Canyon Lodge & Hot Springs, whose deck climbs up the side of the mountain and leads to various small hot tubs. Or visit The Historic Wiesbaden Hot Springs Spa & Lodgings, home of a small, pure hot springs vapor cave. Outside, this spa's mineral swimming pool stretches out below sweeping mountain views. For a unique experience, head to nearby Ridgway for the clothing-optional Orvis Hot Springs. The sprawling gardens and rock-lined pools make this peaceful spot feel like the Garden of Eden.

5 Pagosa Springs

Visitor Center: 105 Hot Springs Blvd., Pagosa Springs; 970-585-1200
visitpagosasprings.com

Pagosa Springs, near the Wolf Creek Ski Area, is where you can witness the world's deepest geothermal hot spring. At 1,002 feet deep, the "mother spring" aquifer is Guinness World Record–certified as the deepest. While you can't go swimming in that pool (it's too hot), it feeds the many baths at the nearby Springs Resort & Spa, Overlook Mineral Springs Spa, and Healing Waters Resort and Spa. The Springs Resort is a sprawling, modern, outdoor wonderland of 24 pools of different temps, sizes, and styles. Across the street, Healing Waters Resort is casual and simple. And nearby is the Victorian-inspired Overlook, with temperature-controlled private tub rooms, a maze of dim indoor pools, and even rooftop tubs.

6 Steamboat Springs

Steamboat Springs Visitor Center: 125 Anglers Drive, Steamboat Springs;
970-879-0880
steamboatchamber.com

Steamboat is famous for its skiing, and it's home to the oldest continuously used ski area in the state, Howelsen Hill. But Steamboat is also a fantastic spot to get warm and toasty. It has about 150 total hot springs, although a few are better known. Strawberry Park Hot Springs is the most beloved, a natural spring set in the mountains, surrounded by trees. Relax in one of the rock-lined pools under the open sky. After dark, Strawberry Park becomes adults-only and clothing-optional. Old Town Hot Springs is a favorite for families, with two waterslides, multiple spring-fed pools, and a climbing wall. Rent a cabana for a private party.

Hot Springs

Pagosa Hot Springs on the hot springs loop

Ski resort in Snowmass near Aspen

COLORADO HAS BEEN CALLED the top skiing destination in North America, and it's home to some of the world's best ski resorts. Overall, the state has nearly 30 ski and snowboarding spots. Some are world famous and busy; others are off the main drag and local favorites. Each boasts its own unique charm, so it's hard to narrow down the best. Ultimately, it depends on what you are looking for. These are not the only slopes to explore, but they give you a taste of your options.

SKI TOWNS

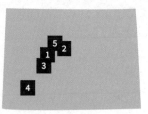

1 Aspen

800-525-6200
aspensnowmass.com

The Aspen Snowmass resort complex in western Colorado is home to one of the most famous ski spots in the world, encompassing four ski areas on four mountains: Aspen Mountain (the oldest), Snowmass (the largest), Aspen Highlands (a bit of a hidden gem north of Aspen), and Buttermilk (home of the X Games and the Red Bull Double Pipe event). Each of the ski areas has its own distinct charm and is worth a visit. For example, while Buttermilk hosts some extreme ski events that are thrilling to watch, this lower-altitude mountain is also ideal for beginners and families. On Aspen Mountain, you can ski where some of the best skiers competed in the World Cup finals. And locals tend to flock to the Highlands because it's less crowded.

2 Breckenridge

1599 Ski Hill Road, Breckenridge; 970-453-5000
breckenridge.com

Head to Breckenridge for low-key, high-elevation skiing (the base of the mountain is 9,600 feet above sea level, with slopes hitting nearly 13,000 feet). Breckenridge is a local favorite, known for being laid-back with an extra-long season, typically from early November all the way into April. "Breck" typically sees more than 350 inches of snow per year on nearly 3,000 skiable acres across five peaks. While the slopes are the highlight, the town itself is worth the drive. The colorful, Victorian downtown is home to festivals year-round, great shopping, tasty restaurants, and craft beer. Breck is a little closer to Denver along the I-70 corridor, which adds appeal for day-trippers.

3 Crested Butte

Crested Butte; 877-547-5143
skicb.com

This small, historic town packs a big punch. Crested Butte is famous for its challenging terrain; these slopes here have hosted several famous skiers and Olympians. But beginners and families can find fun here, too; nearly half of the slopes are suitable for beginner and intermediate skiers. Crested Butte is a bit of a drive—about 4.5 hours southwest of Denver—but the legendary trails (surrounded by 1.7 million acres of national forest), unique restaurants and bars, friendly and quirky community, and scenic drive make it well worth the trek. Crested Butte is considered the last great Colorado ski town for a good reason. Come here for the ultimate ski excursion.

4 Telluride

Telluride; 877-935-5021
tellurideskiresort.com

Shred the snow under blue skies and a shining sun in Telluride, considered one of the best ski resorts in Colorado and North America. It gets more than 175 inches of snow per year on average—and has been known to get more than 300 inches—yet it's almost always sunny. The downside: it's more than 6 hours southwest of Denver, so it's best to hitch a flight to the nearby Montrose Regional Airport or Telluride Regional Airport. The upside of the location: lines aren't as long as they are at ski resorts that are closer to Denver. Runs are a good mix of all levels, from beginner to advanced. If the 2,000-plus skiable acres aren't enough incentive, the adorable, European-influenced, historic town of Telluride and nearby town of Mountain Village make this area a top destination in Colorado.

5 Vail

Vail; 970-754-8245
vail.com

Spanning more than 5,300 acres and nearly 200 trails, Vail is one of the largest and most popular ski destinations in North America. This also means it's one of Colorado's busiest; lines can be long and traffic on the way up I-70 can be grueling. Vail Mountain, located about 2.5 hours west of Denver in the beautiful White River National Forest, sees about 370 inches of snow per year. Beyond the slopes (which Vail claims are the most groomed on the planet), the town of Vail is famous for its luxurious accommodations, high-end restaurants, top-notch service, and European alpine architecture. Along with the elevated lifestyle comes a price tag; it can be expensive to visit here, but if you can afford it, it's a must-do in Colorado.

Ski Towns

Dunton Hot Springs and River Camp

WHAT USED TO BE the shining stars of the gold-rush era
have become abandoned ghost towns. Many of Colorado's former
mining communities have long been vacant, but you can still visit
them today. Some are totally forgotten—just rickety, old structures
in collapse. But others have been revamped, transformed into
museums, and even turned into luxury cabins. Whether you
decide to drive through, walk through, or spend a few days
immersed in this part of Colorado's history, make sure you add
these "ghosts" to your day-trip bucket list.

GHOST TOWNS

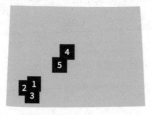

1 Animas Forks

Bureau of Land Management, Gunnison Field Office: 210 W. Spencer St., Gunnison; 970-642-4940
blm.gov/visit/search-details/262787/1

Animas Forks, about 12 miles from Silverton, is one of Colorado's most famous ghost towns, although a four-wheel-drive vehicle is recommended to get there. Off back roads and high in the mountains (at more than 11,000 feet, this is one of the highest-altitude mining camps in the West), you will find a handful of original structures. Buildings here date back to 1873. The highlight: a two-story house called the Duncan House. It's rare to see a multilevel building still standing in an abandoned ghost town. The best way to do Animas Forks is to rent a Jeep and cruise the 65-mile Alpine Loop, a series of dirt roads connecting various small towns in this area.

2 Dunton Hot Springs and River Camp

52068 County Road 38, Dolores; 877-288-9922
duntonhotsprings.com

Live the ghost town life—luxuriously. Dunton Hot Springs is one of Colorado's most interesting ghost towns because this former 19th-century mining settlement has been renovated into luxury cabins with private hot springs access. You can even stay in former miners' homes, which, although revamped, still retain much of their historical charm and authenticity. Service is five-star, and the all-inclusive amenities are excellent, but the cabins aren't overly polished to the point of losing their history. As you walk through this tiny town, it feels like you're in the 1800s. Spend time in the relaxing hot springs, within walking distance of the cabins. The best part is the historically inspired bathhouse. This is by far our favorite way to dive into Colorado's mining background.

3 Silverton

Chamber of Commerce: 414 Greene St., Silverton; 970-387-5654
silvertoncolorado.com

Mining prospectors discovered this area of Colorado in 1860, and with it they found gold and silver along the Animas River. By the 1870s, the town had become a mining camp hub. About a decade later, it was home to a narrow-gauge train. While the miners have since left, the train remains—and it continues to operate, making Silverton one of Colorado's best-known ghost town destinations. The best way to get here is on the scenic train ride (888-872-4607, durangotrain.com) that brings you from Durango to Silverton's colorful, Victorian downtown. This is no dusty ghost town, although you can find abandoned and historical structures. You can stay, dine, and shop here. Silverton is a living, active historical landmark.

4 South Park City

South Park Historical Foundation: 100 Fourth St., Fairplay; 719-836-2387
southparkcity.org

This isn't *that* South Park (the one with a TV show, Stan, and Cartman); rather, it is a ghost town museum in the town of Fairplay. As you wander down these streets and past historically reconstructed buildings filled with memorabilia, you'll feel like you've traveled back in time to the 1850s–80s, when this region saw a gold and silver mining boom. South Park City features 35 authentic buildings (7 on their original sites; the others were relocated) and more than 60,000 artifacts. This unique, open-air ghost town experience, presented by the South Park Historical Foundation, is both educational and entertaining while preserving Colorado's history.

5 St. Elmo

Chaffee County
st-elmo.com

If you can visit only one ghost town in Colorado, pick St. Elmo. This is one of the most visited and best-preserved ghost towns in the state, marked by an abandoned Main Street framed by dusty, wooden structures—even a saloon. Visiting this former gold- and silver-mining destination feels like walking through the Wild West. Back in the 1880s, St. Elmo was home to nearly 2,000 people. Today, people still live here, but it's mainly a tourist spot. Take an off-road vehicle on dirt roads (although you don't need four-wheel-drive to get here; it's easily accessible), go fishing in the creek, and even shop in the general store during the summer. St. Elmo is a quintessential Colorado bucket-list

Ghost Towns

item. *Note:* While in the area, many visitors also stop by Tin Cup, about 45 minutes away. Tin Cup is a ghost town with a wild history. Legend has it that it was run by the cowboy rebels, who scared the sheriffs away.

6 Teller City

About 30 miles south of Walden
tinyurl.com/tellercity

This is a true abandoned ghost town. No one lives here. But you can visit it and get some nice outdoor time while you absorb a bit of history. You can go camping in the nearby Teller City Campground in the small town of Rand, south of Walden. Go on a hike through the looping Teller City Interpretive Trail and look for the remains of what used to be a silver-mining town. It's hard to believe this desolate area used to have hundreds of homes and about 30 saloons. Go here if you want a ghost town adventure without modern restoration. *Note:* You can't visit in the winter, and it has been closed in the past due to the danger of beetle-killed trees blowing down, so check with the U.S. Forest Service before visiting.

Saint Elmo ghost town

Central City

COLORADO IS HOME to 25 National Historic Monuments. Each is worth visiting, but here are a few of our favorite highlights. These sites are ideal for history buffs who want to walk through former mining towns, stroll through Victorian neighborhoods, experience culture in Denver, tour the US Air Force Academy, or see a show in a unique location. Go even farther back in time with an ancient campsite more than 11,000 years old.

HISTORIC MONUMENTS AND BUILDINGS

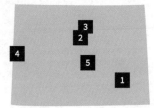

1 Bent's Old Fort National Historic Site

35110 CO 194, La Junta; 719-383-5010
nps.gov/beol

If you're in southeastern Colorado, don't miss Bent's Old Fort, a National Historic Site. Built in 1833 to facilitate trade between Native American tribes and trappers, it was active for only 16 years. But during that time, it played a significant role in history as the only major permanent, white (not controlled by Native Americans or Mexicans) settlement on this stretch of the Santa Fe Trail. It was the heart of the region's trading empire, mainly in the exchange of buffalo robes. The adobe fort was ultimately destroyed and then rebuilt in 1976 as a tourist site.

2 Black Hawk and Central City

Black Hawk: 201 Selak St., Black Hawk; 303-582-5221
cityofblackhawk.org
Central City: 141 Nevada St., Central City; 303-582-5251
colorado.gov/pacific/centralcity

It's a gambling haven in two historic towns in the beautiful mountains. Black Hawk and Central City, a short drive west of Denver, blend together but provide different experiences. Black Hawk is Colorado's biggest gambling town, with more than a dozen casinos, some open 24/7. In Black Hawk you can play blackjack, craps, poker (including tournament poker and cash games with up to $100 per bet), roulette, and all kinds of slots. Head to Central City for a quieter pace but just as much gambling; you can walk (it's only a mile away) or take the shuttle. Smaller Central City features six casinos. There's more in Central City than just gambling, too. See an opera, explore historic buildings, go hiking, grab a beer at a microbrewery, and stay in the area's casino hotels.

3 Colorado Chautauqua

900 Baseline Road, Boulder; 303-442-3282
chautauqua.com

As part of an effort to bring educational and cultural opportunities to the masses in the late 1800s, gathering places called Chautauquas (named after the setting of the first one, on Lake Chautauqua in New York) were started across the country. These assemblies provided classes and lectures, as well as concerts and other social activities. Dating back to 1898, the Colorado Chautauqua is now a National Historic Landmark and the only Chautauqua still standing west of the Mississippi. It is one of the most popular places to visit in Boulder not only for the big-name musicians and speakers that grace its auditorium, but also for its natural setting at the base of the Flatirons, which offer excellent hiking and rock climbing. If you like, you can stay in cottages with historical details and eat in a turn-of-the-20th-century dining hall.

4 Colorado National Monument

1750 Rimrock Drive, Fruita; 970-858-3617, ext. 360
nps.gov/colm

The Colorado National Monument has been called "the heart of the world." It's certainly the heart of Colorado, and one of the most impressive natural sights to see. This monument, not far from Grand Junction, features impressive canyons, red-rock landscapes, and jaw-dropping rock formations, surrounded by wildlife. Visitors enjoy hiking, cycling, camping, or just going on a scenic drive. Start at the visitor center (don't miss the museum inside), and then head out on Rim Rock Drive, a 23-mile, historic route and the only paved road through the monument. You will follow the Colorado River up and down, in and out of the monument. This makes Rim Rock Drive a popular route for cyclists, too. There are several overlooks, so pick up a guide at the visitor center, and have your camera ready.

5 Cripple Creek Historic District

Cripple Creek Information Center: Located in a train car on the corner of Fifth Street and Bennett Avenue, Cripple Creek; 719-689-3289
visitcripplecreek.com

Cripple Creek is one of Colorado's former mining towns that has turned into a dynamic tourist destination. This historic town has been restored so that it feels like you're walking through the Old West, set to the backdrop of mountains. Gambling is legal here, and the town has 10 casinos. You can also go shopping; see a show in the theater; visit the Jail Museum; and explore the outdoors on foot, bike, raft, jeep, or horse. Cripple Creek is a National Historic Landmark; see buildings older than the gold-mining era, including an old courthouse, hotel, church, and two-story hospital.

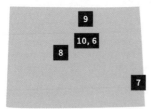

6 Denver Civic Center Neighborhood

Area bounded by Speer Boulevard, Broadway, and Colfax Avenue, Denver

Denver's Civic Center neighborhood is a great place to see early-20th-century and Beaux Arts architecture. In Civic Center Park, see a Greek amphitheater, war memorial, beautiful fountain, and pond. Stroll through the plaza and visit prominent buildings, like the state capitol, the City and County Building, the Denver Public Library, the Denver Art Museum, the judicial building, the municipal offices, and the Colorado state history museum. In addition to being the heart of Denver's public institutions, this neighborhood is where many cultural celebrations take place, from public concerts to vigils to Cinco de Mayo. Civic Center always seems to have some kind of free, public event worth visiting. The neighborhood is also called the Golden Triangle.

7 Granada Relocation Center

Relocation Center: County Road 23 5/10, Granada
amache.org
Amache Museum: 105 E. Goff Ave., Granada; 719-734-5492

After the Japanese attack on Pearl Harbor in 1941, President Franklin Roosevelt used an executive order to force about 117,000 Japanese Americans to relocate, ultimately resettling them in "relocation centers." One such center was in Colorado, near the small, rural community of Granada. The site, called the Granada Relocation Center or Camp Amache, was home to more than 7,300 internees at its peak; over three years, more than 10,000 people passed through the camp. Today, the camp is a National Historic Landmark and on the National Register of Historic Places. You can visit the site, although all but one building has been removed. You can still see the foundation of former buildings and follow signs through the grounds. A walking trail winds through the area. Visit the cemetery, memorial, and museum to learn more. The museum is open five days a week in the summer and by appointment during the school year; call ahead to confirm days of operation.

8 Leadville

Chamber of Commerce: 809 Harrison Ave., Leadville; 719-486-3900
leadville.com

Back in the mining days, the small mountain town of Leadville was one of Colorado's most impressive cities. It was nearly named state capital. Today, it's the highest incorporated city in the United States, at 10,200 feet above sea level, and a fun place to visit for a look at the Wild West. See where Doc Holliday used to sling his guns, stroll through 70 square blocks of Victorian-era buildings, go on a walking tour, and visit one of Leadville's eight museums. A highlight is the National Mining Hall of Fame & Museum, where you can see replicas of mines and mineral collections. Beyond the rich history (quite literally), Leadville is a gateway to the San Isabel National Forest and plenty of outdoor adventure. As for the views, you can't miss Mount Elbert and Mount Massive, Colorado's two tallest mountains.

9 The Lindenmeier Site

Soapstone Prairie Natural Area: 1745 Hoffman Mill Road, Fort Collins; 970-416-2815
history.fcgov.com/explore/lindenmeier

One of the most significant archaeological discoveries in North America lives in northeastern Larimer County, not far from Fort Collins, on what used to be the Lindenmeier Ranch. The area, now known as the Soapstone Prairie Natural Area, is home to the most extensive Folsom-period culture campsite. Prehistoric and Archaic artifacts (mainly, an ancient bison with a man-made spear in it) were found at this site, indicating humans lived here at least 11,000 years ago. Today, the area is protected by the City of Fort Collins. See this ancient site from an overlook, and learn about it via interpretive signs. The Lindenmeier Site is a National Historic Landmark and a great destination for history buffs and outdoor lovers alike.

10 Red Rocks Park and Amphitheatre

18300 W. Alameda Pkwy., Morrison; 720-865-2494
redrocksonline.com

Red Rocks Amphitheatre is a stage like nowhere else on the planet. It is the only naturally occurring, acoustically perfect amphitheater on Earth, famous for its beautiful red rocks jutting upward. Not only does this stage attract the world's top musicians and performers (from the Beatles to the Grateful Dead), but it also has a fascinating history. It's believed the Ute Native American tribe originally used it. In modern society, it has had several different names. It's also a great place to go hiking; Red Rocks has more than 700 acres of open space, including dinosaur bones. Take a history tour in the visitor center.

11 United States Air Force Academy

Visitor Center: 2346 Academy Drive, US Air Force Academy; 719-333-2025
usafa.af.mil

The Colorado Springs area is home to the United States Air Force
Academy, a military organization and university. Visitors are welcome
here, entering through the North Gate from 9 a.m. to 5 p.m. Start at
the Barry Goldwater Visitors Center to learn about the history of the
Air Force Academy and its cadets through films and exhibits. The
campus is filled with beautiful midcentury modern buildings, and
its Cadet Area is designated a National Historic Landmark. There are
several self-guided tours to help you find your way through campus.
You can also walk or bike along the nearby public trails.

Colorado National Monument

Grave of William F. "Buffalo Bill" Cody

HISTORY BUFFS, there are endless educational, historical sites to visit in Colorado. The best place to start is at the History Colorado Center in Denver, which provides an overview of the state's history. Of course, the various National Historic Monuments are also highlights. But beyond that, there are other tourist hot spots worth visiting, even though they don't have the official designation. Here's where to go to be transported back to the gold rush days, for a taste of the Wild West, and for a refined historical experience over a fancy dinner.

MORE COLORADO HISTORY

1 The Buffalo Bill Museum and Grave

987½ Lookout Mountain Road, Golden; 303-526-0744
buffalobill.org

If you're in Colorado looking for a taste of the Wild West, stop by
Buffalo Bill's grave in Golden, about 30 minutes west of Denver. This
museum and grave is a tribute to legendary cowboy William F. Cody,
better known as Buffalo Bill (for his buffalo hunting skills). Learn all
about his life and the Wild West in Colorado through exhibits and
artifacts, such as old firearms, Native American bows and arrows,
historical clothing, and a variety of other interesting finds from back
in the day. This stop is great for people of all ages, history lovers, and
visitors curious about life in the Old West.

2 Fort Carson

El Paso County, Pueblo County, and Fremont County; 719-526-3420
carson.army.mil

Fort Carson, known as the Mountain Post, is a U.S. Army installation
located near Colorado Springs. Camp Carson (as it was called until
1954) was founded in 1942, after Japan's attack on Pearl Harbor.
Today, it's not an open post, meaning you cannot visit unless you
have specific authorization; guests who want to visit unescorted
must first go through a criminal background check. Authorized
visitors will see that Fort Carson has easy access to much of
Colorado's outdoor activities and mountains. Fort Carson has a
population of more than 65,000.

3 Georgetown

Gateway Visitor Center: 1491 Argentine St., Georgetown; 303-569-2405
georgetown-colorado.org

Georgetown, the "silver queen of the Rockies," is a former mining
town and a scenic, fun walk through Colorado's history. It dates back
to a mining camp settled in 1859, during the gold rush. The small
town is perched high in the mountains (more than 8,500 feet above
sea level), and today it's a popular tourist spot where you can see
historical structures. Sites include the Hotel de Paris Museum; the

Alpine Hose No. 2 firefighter museum; and the Hamill House Museum, a restored 19th-century home. While in town, take a gold-mine tour that claims to be the longest walking tour in Colorado. Georgetown has some modern claims to fame, too; it's been in several movies, including *Every Which Way But Loose With Clint Eastwood, The Christmas Gift, Phantoms, Perry Mason: The Case of the Reckless Romeo,* and more.

4 History Colorado Center

1200 N. Broadway, Denver; 303-447-8679
historycolorado.org

The nonprofit historical society History Colorado shares Colorado's history at seven museums around the state, but its flagship museum is the History Colorado Center in Denver. Here you can see permanent and rotating exhibitions, performances, and programs and visit a research center packed with documents, maps, books, photos, and artifacts. The award-winning museum, located in the Golden Triangle Museum District, is a full destination, complete with food, shopping, and 40,000 square feet of interactive exhibits for all ages. History Colorado is also a Smithsonian affiliate, meaning it has access to the Smithsonian's traveling exhibitions and resources.

5 Molly Brown House Museum

1340 Pennsylvania St., Denver; 303-832-4092
mollybrown.org

If you loved the *Titanic* movie and you know the story of the famous ship, you surely know "The Unsinkable Molly Brown," who survived the tragic sinking of the ship. Brown's house in Denver, which has been revamped and turned into a museum, is one of Colorado's most popular historic sites. The Molly Brown House Museum, dedicated to the *Titanic* and Molly Brown, attracts about 45,000 visitors a year. Take a guided tour, see exhibits, and attend educational programs. For something extra fun, look for special events, like a first-class dinner, *Titanic*-style, complete with fancy dishes, live music, and a seven-course meal.

A group of horses running at the Zapata Ranch

SO YOU WANT TO BE a cowboy, baby? You can—at least for your trip, at some of Colorado's most incredible dude ranches. Some Western getaways are luxurious, whereas others are rustic. Ride horses, pet friendly bison, and share campfire tales. You can find cabins fit for a cowboy across all corners of Colorado. Here are a few of our favorites, plus a peek at the American Museum of Western Art, the perfect starting point to round up some history before you transform into Buffalo Bill for a few days.

WESTERN GETAWAYS

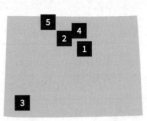

1 American Museum of Western Art

1727 Tremont Place, Denver; 303-293-2000
anschutzcollection.org

See where Colorado's Western heritage blends with art at this unique museum in Denver. The American Museum of Western Art—The Anschutz Collection is filled with art centered around cowboys, horses, and Colorado landscapes. Browse the three-level gallery and find over 600 sculptures and paintings of all styles. The work of more than 180 artists is on display here. You'll gain appreciation for locally inspired art while learning about Colorado's history starting in the early 19th century. Look for special programming throughout the year to enhance your experience.

2 C Lazy U Ranch

3640 CO 125, Granby; 970-887-3344
clazyu.com

Live the life of a cowboy when you stay at this authentic dude ranch about 2 hours northwest of Denver. Immerse yourself in Colorado's ranch country, where not much has changed since the ranch opened in 1919. Here, luxury meets rustic, so you can ride horses and go fly-fishing by day and retreat back for high-end food and well-appointed cabins when your adventures wind down. This family-friendly ranch is all-inclusive, so everything you need is right on site. Keep busy on the 8,500-acre ranch or relax in the spa with some of Colorado's best mountain views. Go on a daily trail ride or stay put in your cabin by the fireplace. C Lazy U is open year-round, and activities adjust with the seasons, from wildflower hikes to snow tubing.

3 Circle K Ranch

27758 CO 145, Dolores; 970-562-3826
ckranch.com

Stay at this fun, relaxed ranch nestled in the scenic San Juan Mountains not far from Mesa Verde National Park. Mesa Verde is especially popular among families, and Circle K Ranch is one of our favorite nearby places for families to stay. In fact, it has been family-run for more than three decades. The lodging is basic, but you won't want to spend much time indoors anyway, because the ranch is home to friendly staff members and friendly horses. The highlight here is a trail ride along the river deep into the woods. Circle K is for travelers looking for a more casual ranch experience. It offers all-inclusive packages, but if you are on a budget, you can customize your experience to meet your needs.

4 Sylvan Dale Guest Ranch

Between mile markers 83 and 84 on US 34, Loveland (see directions on website); 970-667-3915
sylvandale.com

Experience Western hospitality and uncover your inner cowboy at this charming ranch between Loveland and Estes Park, on the way to Rocky Mountain National Park. Sylvan Dale is situated on more than 3,000 acres in the foothills, yet it's close enough to town to be convenient. The well-trained quarter horses are the highlight here. Take them out on a scenic ride across a meadow or up an old wagon trail; Western riding instruction is also offered. If you book a special dude ranch vacation, you get your own horse for the duration of your stay. In addition, guests can hike, fish, participate in ranch chores, relax by the fireplace in a private cabin, and dine on-site. Sylvan Dale has been a popular spot for vacations, weddings, corporate events, and reunions since the 1940s and has been a working horse and cattle ranch since the early 1920s.

5 Vista Verde Guest Ranch

58000 Cowboy Way, Clark; 970-879-6814
vistaverde.com

Vista Verde Guest Ranch is another one of Colorado's top dude ranches, this one located near Steamboat Springs. It offers all-inclusive, luxe amenities, with top-notch service and jaw-dropping views to match. The proximity to Steamboat makes it especially popular in the winter with skiers who also want to hit Steamboat's slopes. Vista Verde makes it easy to plan an outdoor adventure. Activities change seasonally, with sleigh rides, snow tubing, ice fishing, and skiing in the winter, and rock climbing, paddleboarding, and fly-fishing in the summer. Eat s'mores by the fire, go swimming in the pool, indulge in healthy dining, and relax in your cabin. The ranch has unique offerings, too, such as cooking classes and wine tastings. Most of January and early February, and late-August through late-October are set aside for adults-only vacations. The ranch is closed March–June.

6

6 Zapata Ranch

5305 CO 150, Mosca; 719-378-2356
zranch.org

Stay in style at this all-inclusive ranch a short drive from Great Sand Dunes National Park. Zapata Ranch is an active ranch, home to about 2,000 wild bison. Most roam free on the expansive grounds (you can ride a horse right out in the middle of the herd), but one bison named Gordon is domesticated and friendly and will walk up to the fence and eat from your hand or try to snuggle. In addition to exploring the sand dunes, spend time walking through Zapata Ranch's grounds. It boasts one of the most ecologically diverse landscapes in the country. End your day with a delicious community dinner and wine, and then head to the hot tub, surrounded by impressive views of the dunes and mountains.

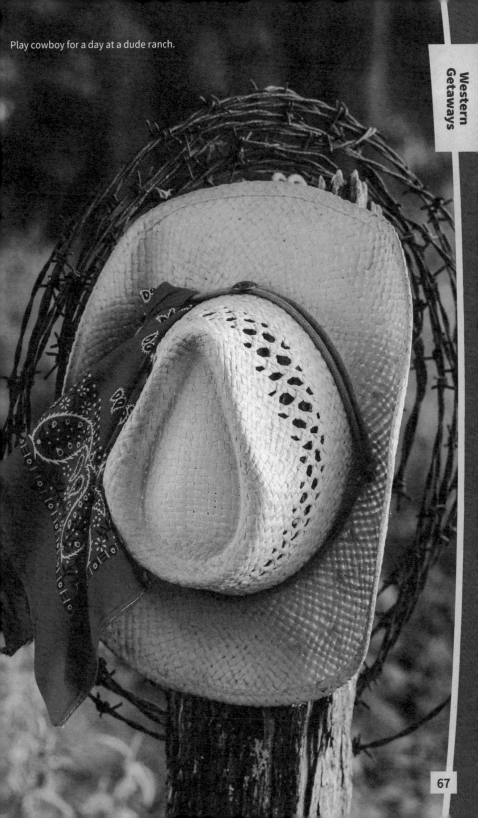

Play cowboy for a day at a dude ranch.

Rocky Mountain National Park

THE BEST WAY to get to know Colorado is face-to-face and
foot-to-gravel, with your shoes on the earth along one of the
state's countless hiking trails. Colorado boasts thousands of miles
of trails, 58 mountains taller than 14,000 feet, and 42 state parks.
It also has 12 national monuments and parks and 13 national
forests and grasslands. The adventure never seems to end. But if
you're looking for a starting point, here are some of our favorite
hiking spots, some simple, some challenging. One thing they all
have in common: views.

HIKING

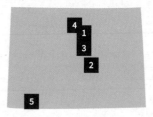

1 Chautauqua Park

Baseline Road and Ninth Street, Boulder; 303-442-3282
bouldercolorado.gov/parks-rec/chautauqua-park

Chautauqua Park, at the base of the Flatirons, is one of the best outdoor activities. The Flatirons' unusual, slanted peaks are the quintessential shot of Boulder. This historic park is packed with outdoor fun and encompasses four peaks; the Royal Arch is a favorite for its dramatic, natural rock arches. Overall, Chautauqua features about 48 miles of trails varying in difficulty and length. A self-guided history hike along the Chautauqua Historic Loop blends the history of this park with a little sweat (moderate–easy, 3.5 miles). For a slightly tougher hike that's short (about 45 minutes), check out the Enchanted Mesa Trail. If you want to add on, continue onto the Mesa Trail. Hiking Chautauqua is like a choose-your-own-hiking-adventure that you can make up as you go.

2 Cheyenne Mountain

410 JL Ranch Heights Road, Colorado Springs; 719-576-2016
cpw.state.co.us/placestogo/parks/cheyennemountain

Cheyenne Mountain towers above the city of Colorado Springs, and as of 2018, you can finally hike all the way to the top. The mountain park itself has 21 trails of various difficulty levels and lengths. But the most exciting trail here is the Dixon Trail, a 9-mile round-trip adventure to the summit and back that passes a plane crash site and offers incredible views of the city. However, this long-awaited trail isn't for everyone; it's rated difficult–extreme, has no pickup points along the way, no camping, and nowhere to refill water. The trail boasts a 2,500-foot elevation gain over 4.5 miles through forest, switchbacks, and rock outcroppings. If you are equipped and up for the challenge, it has become a bucket-list item for athletes in the area.

3 Colorado Trail

Colorado Trail Foundation: 710 10th St., Room 210, Golden; 303-384-3729
coloradotrail.org

The Colorado Trail is called the most beautiful trail in the country. It's a popular, scenic, long-distance trail spanning 486 miles between Denver (Waterton Canyon) and Durango. Try to conquer the whole trail or just a section, depending on your abilities and goals. Hike, backpack, bike, or ride horses through the Rocky Mountains, past five national forests, eight mountain ranges, and six wilderness areas. Most of the trail is high altitude—above 10,000 feet—topping out extra high at 13,271 feet above sea level. This trail, completed in the 1980s, is maintained by volunteers of the Colorado Trail Foundation.

4 Emerald Lake Trail

Rocky Mountain National Park: 1000 US 36, Estes Park; 970-586-1206
nps.gov/romo

If you're looking for a go-to, easy hike with beautiful views in Rocky Mountain National Park, this 3.5-mile round-trip path is for you. Emerald Lake is not far from popular Bear Lake. The path takes you through the forest, providing jaw-dropping views of Longs and Hallett Peaks, Nymph and Dream Lakes, Flattop Mountain, Glacier Gorge, and even a waterfall along the way. The elevation gain is meager (about 600 feet), but it finishes high, at about 10,110 feet above sea level. For such a short and easy hike, the scenic payoff is huge. Take your camera and take plenty of photos.

5 Geyser Spring Trail

San Juan National Forest: 15 Burnett Court, Durango; 970-247-4874
fs.usda.gov/sanjuan

Many visitors may not realize that Colorado has its own geyser. You can see it at the end of the short and moderately difficult hike up Geyser Spring Trail, not far from Delores and the Durango area. The out-and-back trail will lead you through beautiful aspen groves and along switchbacks until you reach Colorado's only true geyser, an icy-blue site that subtly erupts (or more like bubbles) about every 30–40 minutes. It looks like a hot spring, and although it's not too hot, don't be tempted to take a dip, as the noxious gases it emits are more concentrated near the water's surface. The 1.3-mile (each way) hike near the West Dolores River tends to be quiet, remote, and relaxing, and the path is lined with wildflowers, mountain views of the San Miguel peaks, and peaceful meadows. Keep your eyes peeled for old mining areas.

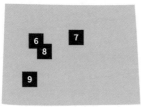

6 Hanging Lake Trail

Hanging Lake Welcome Center: 110 Wulfsohn Road, Glenwood Springs; 970-384-6309
visitglenwood.com/hanginglake

Prepare to be awed by these views. Hanging Lake is an extremely fragile, surreal, bright-blue lake filled by Bridal Veil Falls. Designated a National Natural Landmark in 2011, it's a natural wonder, seemingly suspended off the edge of a cliff and formed by rare deposits of dissolved carbonates. Because of the delicate ecosystem, don't touch the water, try to walk across the logs, or attempt ridiculous selfies that could introduce unnatural elements. Get to this famous destination via the Hanging Lake Trail, a pretty, short trail about 10 miles from Glenwood Springs (a shuttle takes you to the trailhead from Hanging Lake Welcome Center). The trail spans only about 2.5 miles round-trip, but it is steep and rocky. Plan plenty of time to make it up safely and then enjoy the views at the top. Once there, keep going to Spouting Rock for bonus views. This moderate trail has no phone service and can be crowded in the summer, so leave before 8 a.m. and pack water, snacks, and emergency supplies. It's not easy, but it's worth it.

7 Lookout Mountain

Lookout Mountain Nature Center: 910 Colorow Road, Golden; 720-497-7600
visitgolden.com/places-to-go/lookout-mountain

Here's a hike with a view and bonus attractions at the top. At 7,377 feet elevation, Lookout Mountain in Golden is about 30 minutes from Boulder and only 12 miles from Denver. As the name implies, the view of the Great Plains and the Rockies from the summit is Instagram-worthy. But the region has historical significance too; it was originally home to the Ute tribe. At the summit, you can also visit the grave of famous cowboy Buffalo Bill, along with a museum dedicated to his memory. A 1-mile trail connects the museum to the Lookout Mountain Nature Center and Preserve, which has interesting exhibits and nearby trails and picnic benches.

8 | Maroon Bells

Gunnison and Pitkin Counties, near Aspen; 970-945-3319 (Maroon Bells hotline;
call for parking information)
aspenchamber.org/maroon-bells

When in Aspen, you have to explore the Maroon Bells, one of the most
photographed views in the country. This national landmark in the Elk
Mountains contains two of Colorado's most famous mountains, the
Maroon Peak and North Maroon Peak. Due to their closeness to Aspen
(they are about 12 miles southwest), the Bells can get busy with visitors,
so beat the crowds by getting up early for a walk around Maroon Lake.
The Maroon Lake Scenic Trail is easy, short (1.3 miles each way), and
for all levels. For a greater challenge, take on the Maroon Creek Trail;
it's longer (3.2 miles each way) but still doable for many hikers. If you
want to test yourself, head up the Crater Lake Trail. It's shorter than
the Maroon Creek Trail, at only 3.6 miles total, but it's steep and rocky.
Bonus: It's not as busy as the others, so if you're in shape, put in the
extra sweat for better views and thinner crowds.

9 | Ouray Perimeter Trail

Ouray Tourism Office (trailhead): 1230 Main St., Ouray; 970-325-4746
Ouray Trail Group: 970-325-4205
ouraytrails.org

Ouray—a small, charming community built at the base of a bowl
of peaks—is one of the most scenic spots in Colorado, and nothing
compares to hiking around it. Gift yourself some of Colorado's most
inspiring views when you take the Perimeter Trail through the trees,
over a 300-foot-high suspension bridge above the Cañon Creek Gorge
and a waterfall, and through a mountain tunnel. Yes, heights and small
spaces in one. This trail is currently only 6 miles, but construction
continues. It has several forks, where you can choose to turn around
or go farther, depending on the adventure you're up for. It conveniently
starts across from the Ouray Tourism Office. Wear good shoes or hiking
boots, and bring water. Sections get rather steep, with a total elevation
change of about 1,600 feet. Set aside a few hours for the full hike.

Train Ride

COLORADO IS WORLD FAMOUS for its railroad history. The movement has roots in the gold and silver rush in the mid-19th century. Many visitors are surprised to learn some of those original trains still run today. Although they're no longer used for mining, they are popular tourist attractions, bringing passengers on scenic tours of the mountains and into otherwise hard-to-access pockets of nature. Some trains hold special themed events, such as Polar Express–inspired trains around Christmastime. Colorado has a long list of scenic trains; here are a few of our favorites.

TRAIN RIDES

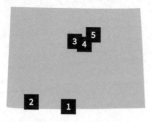

1 Cumbres & Toltec Scenic Railroad

5234-B US 285, Antonito; 888-286-2737
cumbrestoltec.com

You can weave in and out of New Mexico 11 times on the historic Cumbres & Toltec Scenic Railroad. This beautiful steam train leaves from the southern Colorado small town of Antonito and chugs across the Colorado–New Mexico border repeatedly throughout the ride. The coal-fired, steam-operated train was built in 1880 (for mining) and remains the country's most complete example of a late-19th-century narrow-gauge railroad. Today, you can sit back in the car, munch on snacks, and watch the views pass by. Look for a 900-foot gorge, several dark tunnels, and a ghost town along the way. Head out to the open car to get a scent of history; you can smell the coal in the air. Wear sunglasses because fragments of the coal may even be in the air. It's the real deal. The train stops halfway for lunch in Osier. You can then head on to Chama, New Mexico, or back to Antonito.

2 Durango & Silverton Narrow Gauge Railroad

479 Main Ave., Durango; 970-247-2733
durangotrain.com

This is more than a train ride. It's a journey back in time. The five charming, vintage steam trains of the Durango & Silverton Narrow Gauge Railroad, which first began operating in 1882, travel 90 miles between the southern Colorado towns of Durango and Silverton, just as they did back then. Today, the award-winning scenic train isn't used for mining, but rather for views, history lessons, and fun. Traveling in a coach, a parlor car, or an open gondola, passengers get access to views deep in the San Juan Mountains that you just can't get any other way—no cars drive here. The train also offers different packages and events, like Hops and Hops, where kids get to ride with the Easter Bunny and parents get to sip on hoppy beverages.

3 Georgetown Loop Railroad

646 Loop Drive, Georgetown (Devil's Gate Depot); 825 Railroad Ave., Silver Plume
(Silver Plume Depot); 888-456-6777
georgetownlooprr.com

Dating back to 1872, this railroad, one of the state's first visitor attractions, was renowned for its bold engineering. Just 3 feet wide, the narrow-gauge railroad connected the mining towns of Georgetown and Silver Plume, but to do so, it needed to gain more than 600 feet in elevation in just 2 miles. The result: a 4.5-mile winding route of curves, loops, and four bridges across Clear Creek. Today, tourists take the hour-and-15-minute ride for the views and history. About halfway through, you can get off and take an optional tour of the Lebanon Silver Mine, where you can walk 500 feet deep into a mine tunnel from the 1870s.

4 Tiny Town & Railroad

6249 S. Turkey Creek Road, Morrison; 303-697-6829
tinytownrailroad.com

This is a different kind of train experience, one perfect for kids. Tiny Town is a village of more than 100 miniature, to-scale buildings and a kiddie-size railway. Located in Morrison, not far from Denver, this adorable attraction dates back to 1915, when a man named George Turner began building one-sixth-scale buildings for his daughter. Many are precise replicas of famous historical buildings in Colorado. In 1920, he opened her little wonderland to the public, and it instantly rose to become one of the state's most beloved family attractions. In the late '30s, he added a small, 0.6-mile-long railway of open-air cars pulled by a real steam engine that circles the buildings (today there are two steam engines and one diesel engine). Hop aboard every half hour or so. The ride lasts about 10 minutes. Tiny Town is closed October through April.

5 Union Station

1701 Wynkoop St., Denver; 303-592-6712
unionstationindenver.com

Here's a different way to experience trains in Colorado: in downtown Denver at Union Station. This 1914 Beaux Arts station is still a functioning train station and an Amtrak train stop. But the stunning structure is much more than that. In 2014, Union Station underwent a massive renovation and became a destination in and of itself, home to an impressive list of restaurants, shops, and even a hotel. You can stay the night in the Crawford Hotel right in the station and find enough entertainment here to not have to leave for the whole weekend. After you dine, shop, drink, and celebrate, head to the underground bus facility or light-rail station to continue on your journey.

Train Rides

Longs Peak

COLORADO IS HOME TO 58 FOURTEENERS, or mountains that are 14,000 feet or more above sea level. Here are five that rise to the top of many tourists' itineraries. Down south, there's the tallest peak in Colorado (Mount Elbert) and one of the shortest of the fourteeners (Mount Huron, or Huron Peak). Some, like Pikes Peak and Mount Evans, are easy to access; you don't even have to hike to the top of these to claim the views because a road will take you there. For a big challenge in Rocky Mountain National Park, there's Longs Peak. No matter the mountain, make sure you're prepared for the trek—and for the views.

FOURTEENERS

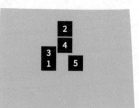

1 Huron Peak

USFS Leadville Ranger District: 810 Front St., Leadville; 719-486-0749
tinyurl.com/mounthuron

If you're worried about altitude sickness but still want to conquer a fourteener, try Huron Peak (also called Mount Huron), which is one of the shortest fourteeners, at 14,003 feet. Although it's not the tallest, it's still considered difficult, can be busy, and is 7 miles round-trip on the Winfield Route. This mountain is known for its outstanding views and wildlife, and the trail is a steady climb that's easy to follow. At the top, look for breathtaking views of the Three Apostles (three slightly shorter peaks). As with all tall mountains, dress in layers, pack snacks and gear, leave early before the afternoon storms, hike in the summertime, and be educated and prepared before you set out.

2 Longs Peak

Beaver Meadows Visitor Center: 1000 US 36, Estes Park; 970-586-1206
nps.gov/romo/planyourvisit/longspeak.htm

Longs Peak is one of Colorado's most famous fourteeners because it's the only one in Rocky Mountain National Park. You will recognize it standing next to nearby Mount Meeker, not a fourteener but only about 350 feet lower. Longs is 14,259 feet, and you can't drive to the summit, although there are different hiking routes of varying difficulty. Warning: They're all tough, long, and are best attempted early in the day (before the afternoon storms) and in warmer months. Trails up the peak include Longs Peak Trail, East Longs Peak Trail, and the Keyhole Route. The latter is technical and requires special climbing equipment. The east face is home to a sharp cliff called The Diamond. Only attempt this hike if you are well prepared, are acclimated to the altitude, and have done plenty of research.

3 Mount Elbert

USFS Leadville Ranger District: 810 Front St., Leadville; 719-486-0749
tinyurl.com/mountelbert

At 14,433 feet, Mount Elbert is nicknamed the "Gentle Giant." That's because while it's the tallest mountain in Colorado and the second-highest peak in the continental United States, it's relatively easy to hike in the summer, if you are well prepared and acclimated to the altitude. There are two popular trails that will take you to the top: the South Elbert Trail (the easiest but longer choice at 6.8 miles, with a 4,800-foot elevation gain) and the North Elbert Trail (tougher but shorter at 4.3 miles, with a 4,400-foot elevation gain). Leave early so you can miss the crowds and the afternoon storms. Snow and hail are likely year-round. For a challenge, there's the Black Cloud Trail, a Class 2 climb with a 5,300-foot elevation gain. This route is extremely difficult even for seasoned climbers, although it's not technical. Mount Elbert is near Leadville in the San Isabel National Forest.

4 Mount Evans

USFS Clear Creek Ranger District: 2060 Miner St., Idaho Springs; 303-567-4382
tinyurl.com/mountevansrecarea

Mount Evans is another impressive fourteener (14,264 feet) that you can summit on foot or by car, and it's easy to access. Take the Mount Evans Scenic Byway just outside of Idaho Springs, west of Denver, and you can check off another bucket-list item; driving up the highest paved road in North America and the fifth-highest in the world. The drive is a bit of an adrenaline rush, with a 9,000-foot elevation gain and plunging cliffs. But it's worth it. You can look out over Denver and beyond. *Note:* It's open only in the summer, and even in the warmest months, the weather here can be moody. Aim to be up early and headed back down well before noon to avoid storms (plus, the earlier you get going, the thinner the crowds will be).

5 Pikes Peak

5089 Pikes Peak Highway, Cascade; 719-385-7325
pikespeakcolorado.com

At 14,115 feet, Pikes Peak is one of Colorado's shorter fourteeners (if a fourteener can be considered short) but is hugely popular due to its proximity to Colorado Springs. In fact, Pikes Peak is one of the most visited mountains in the world. It's one of the easier fourteeners to get to—and you don't even have to hike to get to the top (although you can on a relatively new trail). You can take a bus tour up, hop on a Jeep or Hummer expedition (visit advoutwest.com/pikespeaksummit for details), or drive your own vehicle up. The Manitou and Pike's Peak Cog Railway, the world's highest cog railroad, is currently being reconstructed but is scheduled to reopen in 2021. At the top, don't miss the Summit House restaurant, where you can taste a high-altitude donut. Fun fact: The view from Pikes Peak inspired the song "America the Beautiful." The peak is also a National Historic Landmark and used to be a ski resort.

Dinosaur National Monument

SCIENCE CAN BE a fun center point for a vacation in Colorado. It can lead you to some of the state's most exciting and unique destinations. The Dinosaur National Monument and the nearby town of Dinosaur, Colorado, are a popular pairing for fossil fans. Two of the nation's most famous science centers are located in Boulder and offer family-friendly tours. Families looking for an educational adventure will also love the Fort Collins Museum of Discovery in northern Colorado and the Walking Mountains Science Center in Vail which offers year-round, educational programs that get you outside and exploring.

SCIENCE TOURS

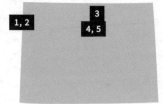

1 Dinosaur, Colorado

visitmoffatcounty.com/dinosaur.php

The tiny town of Dinosaur (population: about 300) is a fun side stop for people visiting the Dinosaur National Monument. While you can't actually view dinosaur bones here, historians believe the prehistoric beasts used to roam these lands, and it's easy to imagine amid Dinosaur's sweeping fields, impressive canyons, and vistas. This historic, Wild West–feeling town is mostly a draw for its interesting name, but that's been its name only since the 1960s. Before, it was called Artesia. Nearby, take a road trip along the Dinosaur Diamond Scenic Byway, and look for the large creatures that now roam the region: elk, wild horses, and deer. Fun fact: Dinosaur, Colorado, is also the home of Marvel villain Molecule Man.

2 Dinosaur National Monument

Canyon Visitor Center: 4545 US 40, Dinosaur; 435-781-7700
nps.gov/dino

This national monument is so impressive that it spans more than 200,000 acres across two states; it is on the border between Colorado and Utah, where the Green and Yampa Rivers meet. It's *the* destination for dinosaur fanatics. Here you can pop up a tent in one of the six campgrounds and explore the many petroglyphs and dinosaur fossils in the area. In the Canyon Visitor Center (on the Colorado side), you can plan out your exploration with books, exhibits, and maps. Then visit the Quarry Exhibit Hall, where you can see about 1,500 dino bones. The Utah side is where you'll see the most dinosaur fossils, and the Colorado side is ultra scenic, with a dramatic canyon. The best view is at Harpers Corner Trail.

3 Fort Collins Museum of Discovery

408 Mason Court, Fort Collins; 970-221-6738
fcmod.org

The Fort Collins Museum of Discovery is one of the state's best family-friendly history, culture, and science museums. It is filled with educational, interactive activities and exhibits, including a Digital

Dome (a large movie screen that stretches onto a rounded ceiling) and an observatory on the roof, where you can get panoramic views of Fort Collins. The main gallery alone is 16,000 square feet of artifacts, fossils, bicycles, and more to teach you about northern Colorado and beyond. The topics of featured exhibits rotate but in the past have included dinosaurs, a history of playgrounds, the solar system, and wildlife. The Exploration Zone turns kids into mini scientists with games that teach scientific concepts, like light and color.

4 National Center for Atmospheric Research

1850 Table Mesa Drive, Boulder; 303-497-1000
scied.ucar.edu

You might not immediately think to visit a research facility when in such an exciting town as Boulder, but truly, NCAR (as it's called for short) is one of the city's coolest attractions, especially for families. The facility is filled with state-of-the-art exhibits and interactive, educational things to do (like "steer" a hurricane, "look" at the sun, and "touch" a simulated tornado). Take a tour, either guided or self-guided using an app, and learn about the atmosphere (and Colorado's crazy weather). Don't miss the art galleries and the educational theater, too. You can spend a whole afternoon at NCAR. After your visit, take advantage of the building's location right against the foothills, with access to great hiking trails and some of Boulder's best views.

5 National Oceanic and Atmospheric Administration and Earth System Research Laboratory

325 Broadway, Boulder; noaa.dsrc.tours@noaa.gov
boulder.noaa.gov, esrl.noaa.gov

Head to the National Oceanic and Atmospheric Administration for more science-y fun in Colorado, this one also stationed in Boulder. Here, scientists study the atmosphere, climate, weather, and air quality. Visitors can tour this interesting facility at 1 p.m. every Tuesday for free (visit boulder.noaa.gov to sign up). You'll see the working lab, check out the national weather forecast (and see where it all starts), and visit a huge, animated globe called Science on a Sphere. Many exhibits are interactive and all are educational. The tours are popular among families, teachers, and researchers. As a bonus, NOAA (as it's called for short) is nestled against the scenic Flatirons. After your tour, head out for a nearby hike and take in the views. You'll see the clouds and sky from a different perspective after the knowledge you'll gain.

6 Walking Mountains Science Center

Nature Discovery Center: Located at the top of the Eagle Bahn Gondola,
Vail Mountain; 970-754-4675
Vail Nature Center: 601 Vail Valley Drive, Vail; 970-479-2291
Avon Tang Campus: 318 Walking Mountains Lane, Avon; 970-827-9725
walkingmountains.org

Explore and learn about nature hands-on through the nonprofit
Walking Mountains Science Center. When in Vail Valley, this is the
best way to learn about the land and connect to the outdoors.
The all-ages, year-round, free, and affordable offerings include
educational programs, youth science camps, seminars, and
interpretive programs. Go on guided hikes, bird walks, evening
beaver pond tours, or wildflower hikes; snowshoe the mountains;
go camping; attend programs led by a naturalist; watch educational
films; ski with a ranger; and more. Walking Mountains has three
locations: the Nature Discovery Center yurt at the top of Vail
Mountain; Vail Nature Center in Vail; and a branch in nearby
Avon. The center serves more than 169,000 students, residents,
and visitors every year.

Green River in Dinosaur National Monument

Steamboat Hot Air Balloon Festival

FESTIVALS CAN BE a fun way to get to know a community, meet people, hear new music, and try new things. It seems every city in Colorado, even down to the tiny towns, has its own annual festivals, from county fairs to microbrew fests to a few, uh, extra-creative ones (you'll find celebrations of bacon, Mexican wrestling and tacos, snow carving, you name it). But among Colorado's seemingly endless calendar of community gatherings, a few rise up as highlights.

ANNUAL FESTIVALS

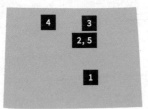

1 Colorado State Fair

1001 Beulah Ave, Pueblo; 719-561-8484
coloradostatefair.com

The Colorado State Fair is the biggest summer event in Colorado. It's even older than the state itself. When the fair was founded in 1869 (Colorado became a state in 1876), it drew about 2,000 people for a horse show in what is today the city of Pueblo. The location has remained the same, but today the fair is much bigger. It spans 11 days of concerts (often featuring big names), rodeos, funnel cakes, horse and livestock shows, a 5K, motorsports, a petting zoo, monster truck rallies, plenty of free events—the list goes on. This fair is such a Colorado institution that in more than 150 years, it has been canceled only once: during World War I in 1917, when the stables were used for the Army National Guard.

2 Great American Beer Festival

Colorado Convention Center: 700 14th St., Denver; 303-228-8000
Brewers Association: 1327 Spruce St., Boulder; 303-447-0816
greatamericanbeerfestival.com

This is *the* big beer event, and not just for Colorado. Some call this the biggest and best beer event in the world. This fall festival features thousands of types of beer from hundreds of breweries around the United States; in the past, it's been more than 4,000 beers from 800 breweries. It's a real bucket-list item, too. The GABF has been crowned one of the best 1,000 places in the country to visit before you die. If you are one of the lucky ones who can snag a ticket (the 60,000-ish tickets sell out instantly, one year in about 20 minutes), you can meet the brewers, eat food, have as many 1-ounce beer samples as you can responsibly consume, watch beer competitions, and shop the merch. The festival is presented by the Brewers Association.

3 Greeley Stampede

600 N. 14th Ave., Greeley; 970-356-7787
greeleystampede.org

While there are many ways to experience Colorado's Western roots, an annual highlight is the Greeley Stampede. This 12-day event has it all: a rodeo, concerts (with big-name bands), a carnival, fireworks, shopping, food, parades, art, a classic car show, and more. The family-friendly event dates back to the late 1800s. It was originally called the Greeley Spud Rodeo and started as a way to celebrate local potato farmers. Back in the 1920s, it drew about 2,500 people. Today, the event attracts more than 250,000 people from around the world, and the associated nonprofit holds other events throughout the year, including golf tournaments and other concerts. But the big summer festival, typically around the Fourth of July, is the highlight.

4 Steamboat Hot Air Balloon Festival

Park at Meadows parking lot, 2310 Pine Grove Road, Steamboat Springs; 970-871-4224
steamboatchamber.com/events/annual-events/hot-air-balloon-rodeo

Every summer, Steamboat Springs unleashes a mass of colorful hot-air balloons for one of the oldest hot-air balloon launches in Colorado. Thousands of visitors go to watch the sky transform into a rainbow of color and fire. (The best place to sit is on the banks of Bald Eagle Lake; bring a blanket.) Balloon pilots participate in fun events, like dipping their baskets into the lake and a Balloon Glow, where a cluster of balloons inflate and glow in unison. After the balloons soar, head to the annual Art in the Park, which coincides with the rodeo. This event features more than 150 different artists and vendors, plus live music and food.

5 A Taste of Colorado

Civic Center Park, Denver; 303-222-5108
atasteofcolorado.com

Foodies, this fest's for you. Head to downtown Denver every Labor Day weekend for one of the state's most anticipated celebrations of all things food. A Taste of Colorado is the state's biggest free food and music festival; more than half a million people come out for the event. Over three days, A Taste of Colorado brings out live, big-name enter-tainment on multiple stages, drinks, a kids area, arts and crafts, and, of course, tons of exclusive food offerings. The festival has deep roots too. It started in 1895 under a different name as a carnival similar to Mardi Gras. It fizzled out by the early 1900s but was revamped in the early 1980s to celebrate the then-new 16th Street Mall. Since then, it has continued growing and was recently named one of the best food festivals in the nation by *USA Today*.

6 Telluride Bluegrass Festival

Town Park: 500 E Colorado Ave, Telluride; 800-624-2422
bluegrass.com/telluride

Telluride is known not only for its skiing but also for its bluegrass. This historic mountain town is home to one of Colorado's biggest annual festivals, the Telluride Bluegrass Festival, hosted by Planet Bluegrass. More than 11,000 music lovers (dubbed "Festivarians") flock to the town every June (during the summer solstice) to jam out to live music outside in Town Park. It's a full event, with camping, plus nearby trails, a pond, playgrounds, beautiful canyon views, and more. While bluegrass is the highlight, you can catch other related genres, too. In the past, bands have included Brandi Carlile, Emmylou Harris, Mumford & Sons, Norah Jones, and Robert Plant, to name a few. The four-day festival is more than 45 years old and always sells out.

An old banjo, often used in bluegrass music

View from Trail Ridge Road in Rocky Mountain National Park

NOT ALL SCENIC VIEWS requires a tough climb. In fact, Colorado is home to many jaw-dropping scenic drives. Most of our favorite routes go up, up, up, sometimes even past treeline. High mountain driving may be a bit scary for some visitors. Hairpin curves, plunging cliffs (sometimes without railings), and mountain traffic can bring on the white knuckles. But at the peak, it's worth it for the bird's-eye views. Here's a closer look at some of Colorado's best panoramas that you can enjoy from the comfort of your car.

SCENIC DRIVES

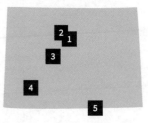

1 Berthoud Pass Summit

US 40 at I-70, about 45 minutes west of Denver
visitgrandcounty.com/explore/mountains-and-vistas/berthoud-pass

If you're looking for amazing mountain views on a well-maintained and accessible road (no four-wheel drive needed and no extreme traffic), head up to Berthoud Pass. The views here are among Colorado's finest, at the top of the Continental Divide and right in the heart of the Rocky Mountains. This high mountain pass features multiple pulloff points where you can stop and take photos or go for a hike and explore the area. It's easy to find: right off US 40 north of where it intersects with busy I-70. Stop here on your way up to visit the popular ski resort of Vail or on your way to Grand County. As with most mountain roads, however, this isn't exactly a leisurely drive in the park. The pass is flanked by pretty steep grades (more than 6%) and the kind of switchbacks that come with mountain driving.

2 Byers Canyon

US 40 between Hot Sulphur Springs and Kremmling
visitgrandcounty.com/explore/mountains-and-vistas/byers-canyon

If you are in the Grand County area, a drive through Byers Canyon will bring the big views. Cruise down US 40 along the rushing Colorado River between Hot Sulphur Springs and Kremmling. The winding drive itself isn't long; the canyon is about 8 miles total, but the best stretch lasts about 2 miles. Enjoy the river, look for wildlife, check out the rock formations on the canyon walls, and keep your eyes open for the train tracks. You might see Union Pacific trains chugging along on their route to Denver. If you don't want to drive yourself, you can take an Amtrak train ride through the canyon. Extend your views and continue throughout Grand County along the Colorado River Headwaters Scenic & Historic Byway.

3 Independence Pass

CO 82 between Twin Lakes and Aspen; 303-639-1111 (road conditions); 970-963-4959 (Independence Pass Foundation) codot.gov/projects/SH82/independence-pass, independencepass.org

If you're visiting Aspen in warm weather, take time for a scenic drive up Independence Pass, part of CO 82. This high mountain road east of Aspen winds all the way up and over the Continental Divide. The pass is one of the best places to witness the colorful changing of the aspen leaves in the fall, right before it closes down for the winter in late October or early November. Another claim to fame: endless views of the Sawatch mountain range. Among the peaks visible from the Independence Pass summit (elevation: 12,095 feet) are Mount Elbert and La Plata Peak, the highest and fifth-highest mountains in the state, respectively. The pass is nearly halfway between Aspen and Twin Lakes, making it not only great for photos but also a useful connection between towns to visit.

4 Million Dollar Highway

US 550 from Ouray to Silverton; 970-247-3500 (Durango Area Tourism Office) durango.org/discover-durango/the-san-juan-skyway

The Million Dollar Highway should be named that for its priceless views. This drive is short (only about 25 miles long, albeit winding), but it's one of the most beautiful road trips in the state and packed with photo-worthy sites along the way. This segment of US 550 in the Durango area of southwestern Colorado will bring you near the mining town of Silverton, with its bright Victorian buildings; the abandoned ghost town of Animas Forks; the San Juan National Forest with 1.8 million acres of natural splendor and adventure; the Box Canyon waterfall; and the charming town of Ouray, with its famous hot springs (see page 37). Enjoy the beauty from your car, or use the drive as a connection between these exciting stops along the way and make a longer trip out of it.

5 Ratón Pass

I-25, 5 miles north of Ratón, New Mexico nps.gov/nr/travel/american_latino_heritage/Raton_Pass.html

Here's a scenic route that is also a National Historic Landmark. You can reach Ratón Pass, on the Santa Fe National Historic Trail, when driving on I-25 between Trinidad, Colorado, and Ratón, New Mexico. The mountain pass itself is perched high, at 7,834 feet above sea level, east of the Sangre de Cristo Mountains, and will take you past volcanic mesas and mountains. At the top, stop at the welcome center, take in the view, and read the interpretive landmark right on the state border. Continue and visit the free Ratón Museum (108 Second St., Raton, NM; 575-445-8979) to learn more about the significance of this drive. Historically, this part of the Santa Fe Trail was considered one of the most important but also one of the most dangerous stretches.

6 Trail Ridge Road

Rocky Mountain National Park: US 34 from Estes Park to Grand Lake; 970-586-1206
nps.gov/romo/planyourvisit/trail_ridge_road.htm

Trail Ridge Road is at the top of many visitors' Colorado must-see lists for its unmatched views. Located in Rocky Mountain National Park, it tops out at more than 12,000 feet above sea level, above treeline. In fact, it is the highest continuous paved road in the country. At the top, you'll find a visitor center where you can learn more about the region. Park here and walk around to take in the views of Estes Park to the east and Grand Lake to the west. *Note:* Trail Ridge Road gets busy in the summer, but it's closed in the winter. Plus, there are sharp turns on steep cliffsides that may challenge some visitors' driving skills, not to mention courage.

Million Dollar Highway (US 550)

Grapevines at a Palisade vineyard, with Book Cliffs beyond

CALIFORNIA GETS LOTS O' LOVE for its wine, but Colorado should be right up there, too. This agriculturally strong state knows how to grow all kinds of fruits, from apples to peaches, and its wine industry boasts more than 140 different producers. Grand Junction and Palisade should be the focus for your wine-cation in the Colorado mountains. Along the Front Range, you can visit a goat dairy, pick your own cherries and apples, or make your way through a corn maze. There are many ways to enjoy Colorado's farms and fields. Here are a few of our faves.

WINE COUNTRY AND FARM TOURS

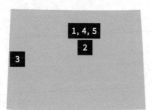

1 Anderson Farms

6728 Weld County Road 31/4, Erie; 303-828-5210
andersonfarms.com

Colorado has millions of acres of farms. In fact, nearly half of the state's 66 million acres are farms and ranches. Many of these farms welcome visitors, especially in the fall, when pumpkin picking and hayrides are popular. One of our favorite farms is Anderson Farms in Erie. Try to find your way out of a huge, 25-acre corn maze (Colorado's longest-running corn maze), take a wagon ride (pulled by an antique tractor) to the pumpkin patch, pet farm animals, and roast marsh-mallows on the campfire. Kids can play on the Pedal Karts and ride the barrel train. At night, adults can test their courage in a creepy Halloween corn maze and the zombie paintball hunt. Everyone gets a kick out of the pressurized pumpkin cannon that shoots pumpkins a quarter of a mile.

2 Denver Botanic Gardens Chatfield Farms

8500 W. Deer Creek Canyon Road, Littleton, CO; 720-865-3500
botanicgardens.org

In addition to the main location in east-central Denver, described on page 20, the Denver Botanic Gardens also operates Chatfield Farms, a 700-acre native plant refuge featuring a meadow, riparian area, lavender garden, historical farm and homestead, functional blacksmith shop, and more. Take a self-guided tour around the farm, and take photos of a restored 1918 dairy barn and silo and an 1874 schoolhouse. Walk along 2.5 miles of trails and look for wildflowers, birds, and wildlife. The farm also holds special events, like the annual Pumpkin Festival and Corn Maze and Santa's Village. (Tip: You can camp at the adjacent Chatfield State Park.)

3 Grand Junction

970-244-1480
visitgrandjunction.com

Grand Junction is known for its stunning natural red rocks, the Colorado National Monument, and endless outdoor activities, from hiking to world-class mountain biking trails to whitewater rafting. But this mountain town in the heart of Colorado's Wine Country is also home to more than 20 wineries. Visit various wineries along the wine trails, do tastings, and prepare to be impressed. Colorado's wines attract international attention. Highlights in Grand Junction include Two Rivers Winery, Whitewater Hill Vineyards, and Graystone Winery. Along the way, you will find some unique varieties, like raspberry-honey blend or cabernet franc. For extra fun, book a guided excursion, like a biking tour through wine country. Just don't drink too much and bike. You don't want a BUI.

4 Haystack Mountain Goat Dairy

1121 Colorado Ave., Longmont; 720-494-8714
haystackmountaincheese.com

Goats and cheese. It's a winning combo for happiness. You can find this and more at Haystack Mountain in the Longmont/Niwot area. This farm makes handcrafted goat cheese old-school style in small batches. When you sign up for a tour of the creamery, you get to learn about how goat cheese is made and sample the artisan cheese. Deepen your experience by visiting the Cheese Education Center, home of the Art of Cheese. Here, you can take hands-on classes on cheesemaking from an award-winning cheesemaker and goat farmer. Don't leave without buying some cheese at the source. You can also buy Haystack cheese at grocery stores and find it at local restaurants and farmers markets. Haystack has a solid reputation; it's been locally owned and operated since 1989.

5 Meadow Lark Farm Dinners

More than 10 farms in Boulder County
farmdinners.com

This is the next evolution of a farm-to-table dinner. It's dinner at the farm. Meadow Lark Farm Dinners organizes and promotes dinners at more than 10 farms throughout Boulder County. At a dinner, the menu is typically based on what was harvested from the fields that day. That means the dishes are a surprise—you won't find an online menu in advance. It also means everything is ultra fresh and often organic. A long table is set outside under the open sky, and you eat the meal overlooking the fields where it came from. Farm dinners take place during the summer only and may include a tour of the farm and a chance to meet the farmers. *Note:* This is such a popular trend that seats are awarded by lottery; sign-up dates are posted on the website.

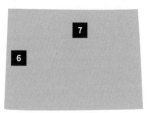

6 Palisade

Palisade Chamber of Commerce: 305 Main St., Unit 102, Palisade; 970-464-7458
visitpalisade.com

Palisade is the soul of Colorado Wine Country. This adorable little town in Grand Valley is known for some of the state's most impressive wineries—over 25 of them. The region's climate (with dry air, cool nights, and plenty of sunshine) is ideal for growing great grapes that are then turned into award-winning wine. Visit the many wineries and taste small-batch and estate-bottled wine. Where you can grow grapes, you can also grow other fruit. Palisade is especially known for its peaches. You can also find farms growing pears, plums, apples, cherries, and more. Visitors enjoy visiting the pick-your-own-fruit farms during harvest season. That's spring for cherries and apricots, summer for those famous peaches, and fall for apples and pears.

7 Ya Ya Farm & Orchard

6914 Ute Hwy., Longmont; 303-485-5585
yayafarmandorchard.com

It's like stepping back in time when you visit the century-old Ya Ya Farm & Orchard in Longmont that specializes in heirloom apples. Here you can pick your own apples, pears, cherries, and flowers in the 8-acre orchard. Make a special event out of it. You can also sip apple cider, try an apple cider donut or apple pie, browse the farm stand, go for a tractor-drawn hayride, and visit with farm animals, including Percheron draft horses, peacocks, chickens, and turkeys. The farm uses organic practices on its 1,000 fruit trees (apple, cherry, plum, and pear), although it's not certified organic. You will also find fresh blackberries, raspberries, and grapes. Best of all, it's free to visit this family-friendly farm (if you are picking produce, you pay a $3 fee plus $12 per half-peck bag). *Note:* You'll need reservations to pick your own apples, and it sells out fast, usually by August.

Palisade

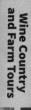

The Ritz-Carlton, Bachelor Gulch from the gondola

VAIL AND ASPEN are synonymous with five-star service, award-winning dining, and high-end accommodations. In fact, Colorado has a wealth (pun intended) of luxurious accommodations that can serve as home base for the most exquisite mountain escape. Many offerings are in the mountains, like Beaver Creek, Steamboat Springs, and farther out in the small town of Gateway. But you can find some of the best food and rooms a short drive from Denver. In true Colorado style, you can even indulge in the good life out under the stars, with a glamping experience that puts many conventional hotels to shame.

LUXURY TRAVEL

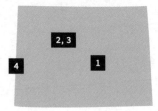

1 The Broadmoor

1 Lake Ave., Colorado Springs; 855-634-7711
broadmoor.com

The Broadmoor is a shining star in Colorado's luxury travel scene. Opened more than a century ago, this Forbes Five-Star resort is a Colorado legend with a long history. The sprawling campus, built around a private lake, feels like its own little town, where everyone greets you with impeccable service. A highlight here is Colorado's only Forbes Five-Star and AAA Five-Diamond restaurant, the Penrose Room, featuring contemporary European fare on the top floor of the South Tower. The resort is also home to one of Colorado's rare Forbes Five-Star spas, one of the best in the nation. Enjoy locally inspired treatments and an oxygen room to counter the altitude. The Broadmoor also has a championship golf course; a nationally recognized tennis program; and other fun perks such as a fly-fishing camp, a 10-course zip-line adventure, and an annual women's Weekend of Wellness. For more of an isolated but equally luxurious getaway, book a night in one of the all-inclusive Cloud Camp cabins, perched on the mountain 3,000 feet above the resort.

2 Collective Retreats

4098 CO 131, Wolcott; 970-445-2033
collectiveretreats.com/retreat/collective-vail

If you want five stars under the stars, these tents are for you. Collective Retreats in Wolcott, about 20 minutes from Vail, has perfected "glamping." That's glamorous camping. In other words, it's all the great things about camping without the inconveniences. Enjoy the solitude and peace of nature, sit out under the stars and enjoy views for eternity, enjoy the embrace of the mountains, and sleep in a tent—with electricity, hot water, luxurious linens, a wood-burning stove, a private restroom with running water, and locally sourced, gourmet food. If desired, book extra activities such as hiking, ATV tours, horseback riding, and whitewater rafting. As if it wasn't already perfect, there's even an on-site winery.

3 Cuvée

Arrabelle Chalet, The Arrabelle at Vail Square, 675 Lionshead Place, Vail;
720-833-4533
cuvee.com

The ski town of Vail is no stranger to luxury, and not just in the form of
Wagyu steaks, expensive cars, and five-star hotels. Vail is also known
for its five-star service, and nowhere better epitomizes that than the
local travel company Cuvée. This company has a portfolio of ultraluxe
penthouses, villas, and estates that you can stay in—properties you
might not otherwise get access to, and with personalized, curated
details. For example, stay in a sprawling, 4,000-square-foot penthouse
in The Arrabelle resort, in the heart of Lionshead Village, just steps
from the gondola. The Arrabelle is one of Vail's rare, true ski-in, ski-out
hotels. The five-bedroom penthouse features crystal chandeliers, a
chef-style kitchen, multiple fireplaces, a wraparound balcony, and
more. Be welcomed by a gourmet charcuterie board, then treat
yourself to dinner prepared by a private chef. Relax with an in-room
massage and yoga session. Cuvée offers multiple Vail properties, as
well as accommodations in Beaver Creek, Colorado Springs, and Aspen.

4 Gateway Canyons Resort and Spa

43200 CO 141, Gateway; 866-671-4733
gatewaycanyons.com

Stay at one of the best resorts in the nation and definitely one of the
best in Colorado at Gateway Canyons Resort and Spa in the red-rock
palisades of western Colorado. It's a bit of a drive from Denver, but this
hidden gem is worth it. It's billed as the world's "first and only discovery
resort." That means it's built especially to feed your curiosity while
traveling; in fact, it was built by the founder of the Discovery Channel.
You'll find educational and adventurous programs in the heart of nature
and surrounded by the finest amenities. Go horseback riding (and learn
to rope cattle), eat dinner outside under the stars, go on an air tour in
the resort's helicopter, and hunt for dinosaur bones, and then return to
your private casita for the night. Gateway Canyons has been named one
of the best resorts in the state by *Conde Nast Traveler*'s Readers' Choice
Awards (it was No. 1 in 2016); the No. 3 resort in the West by *Travel +
Leisure*'s World's Best Awards; and many more.

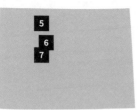

5 Moving Mountains

445 Anglers Drive, Ste. 1-B, Steamboat Springs; 877-624-2538
movingmountains.com

Get access to luxury lodging you could never otherwise experience through Moving Mountains, a family-run luxury vacation rental company. The company can hook you up with Steamboat Springs' most exquisite independent properties, like a penthouse on the Yampa River with direct views of the ski slopes from your private rooftop hot tub. Steamboat is beloved for its skiing in winter, fall color, and biking in warmer seasons (it's known as Bike Town USA). Moving Mountains can set up your whole trip (it's based off the European "catered ski chalet" concept), so you just say what you want to do and the concierge arranges it all, from a private chef to cook you dinner, to reservations at the top restaurants in town, to a trip to the popular Strawberry Park Hot Springs. *Note:* Moving Mountains now has properties in Vail.

6 The Ritz-Carlton, Bachelor Gulch

0130 Daybreak Ridge Road, Avon; 970-748-6200
ritzcarlton.com/en/hotels/colorado/bachelor-gulch

Beaver Creek, a gated town outside of Avon, feels like a private island in the midst of Colorado's best ski terrain. Overlook it all when you stay at The Ritz-Carlton, Bachelor Gulch, which feels like a stone castle on the hilltop. This ski-in/ski-out resort is consistently recognized as one of the country's best hotels and one of the state's premier ski spots, and for good reason. In addition to the impressive hospitality, you can find Vail Valley's only cigar lounge, a year-round outdoor heated pool with views of the ski slopes, penthouses with full kitchens and living rooms, and one of Colorado's best spas. A highlight of the world-class spa is the coed grotto with waterfalls, where you can sip fruit-infused water after a long day on the slopes.

7

The St. Regis Aspen Resort

315 E. Dean St., Aspen; 970-920-3300
marriott.com/hotels/travel/asexr-the-st-regis-aspen-resort

Aspen is world famous for luxury. The best of the best can be experienced at The St. Regis Aspen Resort, a mountainside manor located just steps from the ski slopes (right between Aspen Mountain's two main ski lifts) and shopping and restaurants downtown. Suites come with a personal butler, who will unpack and pack your suitcases, iron your clothes, and bring you fresh coffee in the morning. Ask about having the Bloody Mary bar sent to your room. Rooms here have marble bathrooms, bespoke Ralph Lauren furnishings, and Frette linens. Every day, the hotel hosts a sunset champagne sabering, where a bottle is popped and the evening is toasted. Make sure you visit the Remède Spa (we recommend a customized facial) and Velvet Buck, the resort's top-of-the-line restaurant. After a busy day, cuddle up by the fire with a book and cocktail in the Astor Library.

Luxury Travel

UFO Watchtower

ONLY IN COLORADO CAN you look for aliens in an "energetic vortex" and then visit a farm of alligators. Colorado is packed with odd attractions. If you like history, the Carousel of Happiness will whirl you around, or hop on another of the country's best-preserved antique carousels. If your idea of a roadside attraction includes the supernatural, book a night at the haunted Stanley Hotel. Then there are the only-in-Colorado stops that are also rites of passage: a visit to Casa Bonita, the "Mexican Disneyland"; dinner at The Sink, where you can order the same pizza as former president Obama; or a photo-op on the mile-high step at the capitol building.

ODDITIES AND ROADSIDE ATTRACTIONS

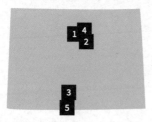

1 Carousel of Happiness

20 Lakeview Drive, Nederland; 303-258-3457
carouselofhappiness.org

Pick one of 56 hand-carved animals for your ride on the whimsical Carousel of Happiness in the mountain town of Nederland outside of Boulder. This colorful carousel was built on a restored 1910 carousel frame, complete with the tunes of a 1913 Wurlitzer organ. It's inexpensive to ride: only two bucks a whirl. The carousel itself has an interesting story. In its original incarnation, it was the only attraction to survive a large park fire, and it made it through a huge windstorm that blew a roller coaster onto the carousel. Today, there are only about 150 wooden carousels still in existence in the United States. In addition, the man who bought and revamped the carousel was inspired by a music box he held to his ear when he served in Vietnam as a young Marine. To distract him in war, he imagined a carousel in the mountains, which he spent 26 years bringing to life.

2 Casa Bonita

6715 W. Colfax Ave., Lakewood; 303-232-5115
casabonitadenver.com

Go to this legendary Mexican restaurant for the "eater-tainment," not for fine dining. Casa Bonita, also known as Mexican Disneyland, has been a Colorado staple for more than four decades. It's been named one of the nation's best roadside attractions, and there was even a *South Park* episode based on it. This family-friendly destination offers all-you-can-eat Mexican food (although save your appetite for the free sopapillas at the end; they're really the only food worth eating). But Casa Bonita is more about the 30-foot waterfall, 14-foot-deep pool, cliff divers, magic and puppet shows, roaming mariachi musicians, arcade games, fake gunfights, and dark, "spooky" cave. This Lakewood historical landmark is the last standing branch of an old chain. Today, it's simultaneously an ironic cult icon among grown-up natives, as well as a wonderland for kids. The line to get in is usually long, but think of it as an amusement park. And wait for a table by the waterfall. Or if you're a *South Park* fan, ask for the *South Park* table. It's upstairs under a golden dome facing the waterfall.

3 Colorado Gators Reptile Park

9162 County Road 9 N., Mosca 719-378-2612
coloradogators.com

Alligators? In Colorado? Oh, yes. Hundreds of them. They all live at the
Colorado Gators Reptile Park. Of course, they aren't naturally here.
As the story goes, in 1987, the owners of a fish farm bought 100 baby
alligators to eat leftover tilapia. The region's warm geothermal water
was perfect for alligators, and the babies grew and thrived. Today, the
fish aren't the draw. Tourists come from all over to check out the gators
and other reptiles, such as pythons, tortoises, and iguanas. There are
even a few scaly celebrities here, including Morris, who appeared in
Happy Gilmore. You can also hold a baby alligator, buy feed to toss at
the gators, pet tortoises, and learn about reptile rescue. The property
also includes a working fish farm, and catch-and-release fishing is free
with admission.

4 Frozen Dead Guy Days

Nederland; 303-506-1048
frozendeadguydays.org

This one's odd, even for Boulder. Frozen Dead Guy Days, in the small
mountain town of Nederland just outside of Boulder, is exactly what
it sounds like: a community celebration of, well, a frozen dead guy.
True story: A man named Bredo Morstoel is cryogenically preserved in
a shed above Nederland, and the wildly popular annual festival pays
homage to his unusual request. It features dozens of live bands and
things like coffin racing, a parade of hearses, and Cryonic Blue Balls
Punch. As much as the event is about death, it's also about winter, and
ultimately hope for a new life after the thaw. So there are also frozen
T-shirt contests, a polar plunge into icy water, frozen turkey bowling,
ice carving, and the crowning of an Ice Queen. It's a little macabre, a
lot of fun, and easily one of the quirkiest celebrations in the country.

5 Indiana Jones Bed and Breakfast

502 Front St., Antonito; 800-497-5650
indianajonesbedandbreakfast.com

You can stay at the childhood home of Henry Jones Jr. You know,
Indiana Jones. The house where the beginning of the movie *Indiana
Jones and the Last Crusade* was filmed is in the tiny town of Antonito
in southern Colorado, near the New Mexico border. Today, it's an
adventure-themed bed and breakfast. You'll know it's the place by the
mailbox out front with the name Jones on it, just like in the film. Book
your stay in advance. The two-level, historical house has limited space:

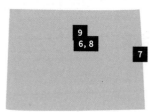

three rooms upstairs and one on the main floor. Each room has a themed name, like The Crusader and The Coronado. Indy fans will also recognize the nearby Cumbres & Toltec Scenic Railroad train from the movie. Remember a boy hiding in a circus train, crawling through a car of snakes? That was filmed here, too.

6 International Church of Cannabis

400 S. Logan St., Denver; 303-630-9500
elevationists.org

To some Coloradans, cannabis is more than a legal drug for people 21 and older. It is sacred. That's what members of the International Church of Cannabis in Denver believe. This nondenominational church of "Elevationism" was founded in Denver by people who wanted a new kind of spiritual outlet and a home to come together to improve themselves and search for meaning, with help from ritualistic, mindful cannabis use. Here, Elevationists regularly gather to partake in their sacrament (use cannabis), which they see as a gift from the universal creative force. To join the church, submit an application for membership and you can get access to the space and the gatherings. The church also conducts weddings. There are certain visiting hours for nonmembers, too, but cannabis cannot be consumed during these hours.

7 Kit Carson County Carousel

Kit Carson County Fairgrounds: 815 N. 15th St., Burlington; 719-346-7666
kitcarsoncountycarousel.com

This historic carousel dates back to 1905 and was the sixth of 74 carousels made by the Philadelphia Toboggan Company. (Nearly 2,500 wooden carousels were made nationwide until the 1930s, but fewer than 150 remain.) This carousel is one of the best preserved and is fully operational. It's the only antique carousel in the country still with original paint on both the animals and the scenery. It's also the company's only surviving menagerie (meaning it has animals besides horses). This special ride was originally bought for Elitch Gardens, an amusement park in Denver. But Elitch's wanted an upgrade in the late 1920s, so the theme park sold the old carousel to Kit Carson County, where it remains functioning today. Now known as the Kit Carson County Carousel, this ride has three rows of animals and was designed to go faster than a regular carousel: more than 10 miles per hour. It's a fun, rare ride through history.

8 Mile-High Marker on the State Capitol Steps

Colorado State Capitol: 200 E. Colfax Ave., Denver
colorado.gov/capitol

When in Denver, it's a Colorado bucket list activity to visit the Colorado state capitol building and look for a marker on one of the granite steps leading up to the entrance. The 13th stair is supposedly exactly 5,280 feet above sea level, or 1 mile high, and it bears a marker boasting its height. This altitude is why Denver is called the Mile High City, although technically the city itself isn't quite a mile up. This stair is, though. Probably. For now, at least. Over the years, a handful of stairs have been coined the special spot. First, it was the 15th step. You'll see an engraving on this step designating it ONE MILE ABOVE SEA LEVEL. But in 1969, students remeasured and claimed it was actually the 18th step, and that step was marked with an update. But then in 2003, researchers did more measurements and issued yet another correction: the lucky 13th step. Maybe take a selfie on all three steps, just in case it changes by the time you get home.

9 The Sink

1165 13th St., Boulder; 303-444-7465
thesink.com

When in Boulder, you must eat at The Sink on University Hill. It's been around for nearly a century, has multiple ties to celebrities, and is colorful and quirky. The walls and ceilings are covered in murals, cartoons, and graffiti. Not to mention the food. Although it's far from health food, The Sink is considered one of Boulder's best pizza and burger joints. Pick from more than 10 specialty burgers, or opt for the food of the famous visitors. Food Network chef Guy Fieri's pick when he ate here: the Texas Onion Straw burger, the Buddha Basil pizza, and the Cowboy Reuben. TV personalities and chefs Anthony Bourdain and Eric Ripert had the Texas Onion Straw burger, a portabella burger, and Kansas City barbecue short ribs. Or eat what former president Obama ordered: a pizza with pepperoni, sausage, black olives, green peppers, and red onions. Formerly called the Sinkza pizza, it has since been renamed the P.O.T.U.S. Request to sit at table 54 to see pictures of Obama's visit. Oh, and actor Robert Redford used to work as a janitor here. Before you leave, write your name on the wall. At The Sink, that's not vandalism; it's a rite of passage.

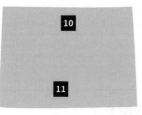

10 The Stanley Hotel

333 Wonderview Ave., Estes Park; 970-577-4040
stanleyhotel.com

Ghost hunters and Stephen King fans alike seek out the famous Stanley Hotel in Estes Park, a small, historic town just outside Rocky Mountain National Park. This supposedly haunted hotel is best known for inspiring King to write *The Shining*. The sprawling white hotel plays into its reputation with a nighttime ghost tour that brings you into tunnels below the hotel. Request to stay in rooms 217 (where King is said to have stayed) or 401; both which are said to have the most paranormal activity. The Stanley holds special events year-round, especially around Halloween, such as the annual Shining Ball, with tributes to the book and movie. Beyond the spooky reputation, the hotel itself is elegant and historic, with dramatic chandeliers and gilded mirrors.

11 UFO Watchtower

CO 17 (2.5 miles north of Hooper), Center; 719-378-2296
ufowatchtower.com

Many of Colorado's quirkiest attractions are down south, especially in the San Luis Valley. UFO fanatics—and 15 psychics—say that's due to the presence of two large energetic vortexes in the area, which they say has led to an extraordinary number of alien-sighting reports. Hence the UFO Watchtower, where a small domed building containing a gift shop sits beneath a simple metal observation deck. Many visitors leave gifts for alien visitors outside in the "garden": piles of photos, toys, letters, coins, trinkets, and other personal objects. Even if you don't leave behind an offering or believe in aliens, the 360-degree mountain view from the deck is lovely. You can even camp here year-round for cheap. Just drop money in the green box on the tower.

Colorado Gators Reptile Park

Boulder Dushanbe Teahouse

COLORADO IS FOR FOODIES, and the dining options seem limitless. But a handful of restaurants really stand out, some for their innovative dishes and award-winning chefs, and others for their interesting menu options. If you're in Denver, a great place to start to get a taste of Colorado is in Larimer Square, where we've provided an all-day foodie tour you can tackle if your belly is extra ambitious. Other highlights include an upscale steakhouse with a football legacy; an artistic teahouse; and high-end dining with a view. For some Colorado specialties, try the Mountain Pie at Beau Jo's and the Rocky Mountain oysters at Bruce's (hint: they're not oysters).

FOODIE HIGHLIGHTS

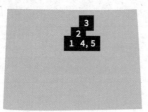

1 Beau Jo's

1517 Miner St., Idaho Springs; 303-567-4376
beaujos.com

You've heard of Chicago-style and California-style pizza. But have you conquered a Mountain Pie? Beau Jo's is the originator of the Colorado-style pizza. These pies are monstrous—nay, mountainous. One of these thick-crust pizzas can feed an entire hungry family. The dough is made with local honey instead of sugar, and you'll find bottles of honey on the table to dip the fat, braided crust in. The crust is thick so it can hold a mega amount of toppings. It's common to get a pizza that weighs 5-plus pounds. As Beau Jo's knows, the Colorado lifestyle is active. The Mountain Pie is built to refuel you. Beau Jo's started more than 40 years ago in Idaho Springs and now has six locations across the state.

2 Boulder Dushanbe Teahouse

1770 13th St., Boulder; 303-442-4993
boulderteahouse.com

It's hard to decide which is more incredible: the food, the architecture, or the history of this famous teahouse on Boulder Creek. The colorful, artistic building was a gift to Boulder from its sister city, Dushanbe, Tajikistan. Dozens of artists in central Asia built the restaurant by hand using ancient techniques (no power tools), then disassembled and sent it to Boulder, where it was reassembled. As you enjoy your tea and Asian food, you will be awed by intricate, Persian-style details and a hand-painted and hand-carved ceiling. In the middle of the room: a central pool surrounded by seven hammered-copper sculptures. Outside: an elaborate flower garden where you can dine in warmer weather. The building is a true, one-of-a-kind work of art. In addition to ethnic food and a long tea list, the Boulder Dushanbe Teahouse also offers special events, like tea parties, afternoon tea, and workshops.

3 Bruce's

123 First St., Severance; 970-686-2320
brucesbar123.com

Not all bucket-list-worthy restaurants are fancy. In fact, this one might be more of a dare. Or a rite of passage, depending on your perspective. Bruce's is famous for serving a, uh, delicacy of the West: Rocky Mountain oysters. But these aren't oysters. Nope. They're bull testicles, often served deep-fried. Bruce's has been serving 'em up hot since 1959, and this has helped shape the small town of Severance. In the middle of town, you'll see a sign: THE TOWN OF SEVERANCE: WHERE THE GEESE FLY AND THE BULLS CRY. For a challenge, hit up Bruce's on the all-you-can-eat nights or join the annual Nut Run event. For a taste test, order the Oysters Combo, which features bull, buffalo, and lamb "oysters." You can even order frozen ones to take home. If this Colorado culinary tradition turns your stomach, you can always try another unique menu item here: a yak burger.

4 The Cherry Cricket

2641 E. Second Ave., Denver; 303-322-7666
cherrycricket.com

The Cherry Cricket in Cherry Creek (and another branch in the Ballpark neighborhood in Denver) is a longtime Denver icon. This is where to get the best burgers in Denver. You know they're the best because you can build your own. The ever-packed burger joint has been popular since 1945, when it opened, and was one of Denver's first sports bars in the 1960s, when it was owned by Bernard Duffy, who added the now-vintage sign. The casual, modest restaurant sticks out among the fine dining and upscale shopping in Cherry Creek, and that uniqueness is what makes it so beloved. While the area continues to grow, this bar seems suspended in time. The Cherry Cricket still feels like an old-fashioned, friendly, neighborhood bar slinging tasty burgers and cold beer. No gimmicks or trends; just tried-and-true flavor. As for the name of the restaurant? No one knows what it means or where it came from. Which is oh so Cherry Cricket.

5 Elway's

1881 Curtis St., Denver; 303-312-3107
elways.com

When in Denver, Broncos fans *have* to eat at a restaurant named after former quarterback John Elway. But even if you aren't a football fan, you'll enjoy the fine cuts of steak in a gorgeous space. Elway's has four locations, all in Colorado: Cherry Creek, the Denver International Airport, Vail, and downtown Denver (in The Ritz-Carlton). Downtown's

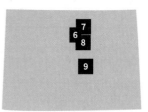

restaurant has a fantastic lounge and outdoor terrace. USDA Prime, hand-cut steaks are the star of the menu here. But you can also find fish, local lamb, a raw bar, and dishes that change seasonally. Elway and a friend of his founded the restaurant with the hope that it would embody the many aspects of Colorado, offering a fun, adventurous, celebratory, relaxing, and vibrant atmosphere. Add to that a solid wine list in a sophisticated yet unpretentious atmosphere, and Elway's is a top spot for a special event or impressive date in the heart of downtown.

6 Flagstaff House

1138 Flagstaff Road, Boulder; 303-442-4640
flagstaffhouse.com

The best views from a table in Colorado. Five-star service. A wine list to impress the most discerning of connoisseurs. You can find all three at the Flagstaff House in Boulder, a New American/French, family-run restaurant with more travel and dining awards than any restaurant on the Front Range. And it's no wonder—the view is not only reason enough to make this a must-stop while in Boulder; it's reason enough to *go* to Boulder. It is built atop Flagstaff Mountain, 6,000 feet high, with views that go on forever. The menu and service match the jaw-dropping views, as does the wine list: the wine cellar is filled with over 16,000 bottles, including more than 30 Dom Pérignon vintages. Fresh, innovative dishes rotate constantly and are reliably tasty. You should expect no less, as Flagstaff's executive chef, Chris Royster, won an episode of Food Network's *Chopped*.

7 Johnson's Corner

2842 SE Frontage Road (Exit 254 off I-25), Johnstown; 970-667-2069
johnsonscorner.com

If you're on a road trip and craving some comfort food, gas station food normally won't do. But this is no ordinary gas station: the retro, family-run diner has been named the best truck-stop restaurant in the country and was featured as such on the Food Network, in addition to a long list of other accolades. Opened in 1952, it's one part restaurant, one part roadside attraction. The stars of the menu here are the massive, gooey cinnamon rolls that are as big as your plate. Taste these "world famous" pastries 24 hours a day on Fridays and Saturdays (and 5 a.m.–11 p.m. the other days). A cinnamon roll will more than fill you up, but the menu also features classic, home-style comfort food, pie, and especially tasty breakfast. After licking the frosting off your finger-tips, you can shop in the attached store, get some souvenirs and road snacks, fill up your gas tank, and continue your Colorado adventures.

8 | Larimer Square

Larimer Street from 14th to 15th Sts., Denver
larimersquare.com

Plan an all-day foodie tour through Denver's most historic block, Larimer Square. Start with brunch at Tamayo (1400 Larimer St., eattamayo.com), some of the best Mexican food in Denver. Score bottomless mimosas, Bloody Marias, and margaritas to pair with plates of Modern Mexican brunch specialties. For lunch, don't miss Rioja (1431 Larimer St., riojadenver.com), James Beard award–winning chef Jennifer Jasinski's restaurant featuring imaginative Mediterranean dishes and Spanish wines. Tip: Try the handmade pastas. For happy hour, check out Crú Food & Wine Bar (1442 Larimer St., cruwinebar.com) for a wine flight and paired appetizer, or toast with a glass of champagne at Corridor 44 (1433 Larimer St., corridor44.com). Then enjoy a romantic dinner at chef Jasinki's Bistro Vendôme (1420 Larimer St., bistrovendome.com), tucked away in a cozy courtyard. If romance isn't on your plate, opt for dinner at the chic urban restaurant Tag (1441 Larimer St., tag-restaurant.com), with cross-cultural culinary options you can enjoy inside or out. Wrap up your epic foodie tour at the Crimson Room's unique, intimate space (1403 Larimer St., thecrimsonroom.com) for late-night jazz comple-mented by a signature cocktail and exquisite sweets.

9 | Penrose Room

1 Lake Ave., Colorado Springs; 719-577-5733
broadmoor.com/dining/penrose-room

The Penrose Room is Colorado's only Forbes Five-Star and AAA Five-Diamond restaurant. Perched on the top floor of the South Tower at The Broadmoor hotel, it overlooks the resort and the mountains to the west and Colorado Springs (and beyond) to the east. The service is unmatched; each table gets its own three-person team, plus the som-melier. Plan to stay awhile in this elegant restaurant, as it serves only a multicourse prix fixe or chef's tasting menu that changes seasonally. Expect fine seafood, local meat, foie gras, fresh salads, and produce perfectly paired with wine from a lengthy list. The restaurant also features live music in the center of the room, and you're welcome to get up and dance after you dine—or between dishes to make space for impressive desserts crafted by a master executive pastry chef.

Larimer Square

SKIP THE CHEESY souvenir shops and head straight to the heartbeat of Colorado's shopping scene. From high-end boutiques to fashion shows, Colorado's style quotient continues to grow. There's a little something for any shopping bag, too, whether that's some fancy pants for your dog or an only-in-Colorado gift to bring home. In true Colorado spirit, our favorite shopping destinations are also rife with people-watching, nearby entertainment, and tasty restaurants to keep you fueled. Spend time browsing the outdoor shopping districts, or explore some unique experiences at the Stanley Marketplace or the Denver Pavilions.

SHOPPING DISTRICTS

```
    4
  1-3, 5
```

1 Cherry Creek

Cherry Creek Shopping Center: 3000 E. First Ave., Denver; 303-388-3900
shopcherrycreek.com
Cherry Creek North: 2401 E. Second Ave, Denver; 303-394-2904
cherrycreeknorth.com

Cherry Creek is the heart of Colorado's luxury shopping and fashion. Here you will find two main shopping areas: Cherry Creek Shopping Center (the mall) and Cherry Creek North. Cherry Creek Shopping Center features more than 160 shops, including 40 exclusive retailers, many of which are high-end (such as Tiffany & Co., Burberry, and Louis Vuitton). You can also find typical shopping-mall anchors, as well as some popular dining options. Nearby, you will find the 16-block Cherry Creek North shopping and dining district, which is rich with boutiques, restaurants, galleries, spas, and more. The area is made for art lovers, luxury shoppers, and people seeking unique fashion and home goods. After a day browsing the storefronts, you can dine and even stay in the area, making Cherry Creek a total day-trip destination.

2 Denver Pavilions

500 16th St., Denver; 303-260-6001
denverpavilions.com

The Denver Pavilions is often lumped in with the 16th Street Mall (after all, this shopping oasis *is* on the mall), but we think it's a distinct destination in and of itself. The open-air mall features more than 40 stores and restaurants on multiple levels. Here you will find great local shops and reputable chains, as well as popular restaurants and bars. Non-shoppers have plenty of entertainment options, including a hip bowling alley, a 15-screen movie theater, and the Hard Rock Cafe. A bonus: Parking is easy to find, as the Pavilions features an underground parking area. When on the 16th Street Mall, make sure you set aside plenty of time to explore the Denver Pavilions.

3 Larimer Square

1430 Larimer St., Denver
larimersquare.com

Whether you're stationed in Denver or headed back from the mountains, Larimer Square is a must-visit stop for shopping. You can find regionally exclusive, upscale fashion boutiques, such as Moda Man and Hailee Grace; a "clean" beauty boutique, Aillea; accessory specialists, such as Fluevog shoes and Goorin Bros. hats; and even a hookup for your Colorado Western wear (howdy, new boots) at Cry Baby Ranch. There are plenty of quirky destinations, too, like a high-end store and spa for pets called Dog Savvy Boutique. In the fall and spring, Larimer Square puts on a fashion show that features the latest styles from the area's retailers, drawing fashionistas from across the state.

4 Pearl Street Mall

1942 Broadway, Boulder; 303-449-3774
boulderdowntown.com

The Pearl Street Mall is like a fairy tale: brick-lined streets with the backdrop of the Flatirons, talented buskers filling downtown with music, the scent of garlic and fresh-roasted coffee beans. In the winter, the four-block pedestrian mall glows with twinkling white lights. Home to some of Boulder's best local (and chain) shops and restaurants, Pearl Street is Boulder's heart, and as such, it's quirky, spirited, and one of the state's most hoppin' tourist destinations. In fact, it has been named one of the nation's best open-air pedestrian malls. It's home to more than 200 businesses, most of which are local. You'll find talented jewelers and artisans, fashion boutiques, bookstores, pop-up shops, art galleries, and more. Pearl Street can entertain you for a full day or much longer; you'll want to stay awhile.

5 16th Street Mall

16th Street between Wewatta and Broadway Streets., Denver; 303-534-6161
denver.org/things-to-do/denver-attractions/16th-street-mall

This outdoor pedestrian mall is in the bull's-eye of downtown Denver. It's lined with stores, restaurants, and bars and offers Denver's best people-watching. You can stroll along the 1.1-mile stretch, ride the free electric shuttle, or hop aboard a horse-drawn carriage or pedicab. There's always something happening, from buskers performing to organized festivals, like the 16th Street Fair in the summer. The mall has been a Denver attraction for more than three decades. The street connects LoHi in the north to the Denver Pavilions shopping complex in the south. After shopping, relax outside with a drink and snack; it's usually easy to find a patio table, since there are more than 40 outdoor cafés.

6

6 | Stanley Marketplace

2501 N. Dallas St., Aurora; 720-990-6743
stanleymarketplace.com

The Stanley Marketplace is a unique, community-centric marketplace that puts Aurora on the map for a fun day trip. This former aviation facility has been converted into a hip warehouse packed with more than 50 independent businesses, from food vendors (hello, CBD donuts) to a brewery, a nail salon, a barbershop, a yoga studio, and shopping galore. The Stanley is hyperlocal; it's the best of Colorado under one roof, and you can easily spend a full day there. Start with brunch at Annette Scratch to Table, helmed by a James Beard nominee, which features a seasonally changing menu in an intimate dining hall. Then shop for clothes for yourself, and find educational toys and let your kids create in the MindCraft makerspace. And don't miss Zero Market, which sells sustainable home products that encourage less waste. A highlight at the Stanley is the Infinite Monkey Theorem taproom, located in the former Stanley Aviation break room and decorated with vintage furniture and conversation pieces.

16th Street Mall

Colorado Rockies

COLORADO HAS BEEN NAMED one of the fittest states, so it's no surprise that it is also home to some of the best professional sports teams. Leading the way is the Denver Broncos, with multiple Super Bowl wins; the Colorado Rockies baseball team; the Denver Nuggets basketballers; and the Colorado Avalanche, a pro ice hockey team. Of course, the college sports teams are also huge draws. Leading the excitement is football (and other sports) at cross-state rivals University of Colorado and Colorado State University.

SPORTS

1-5

1 Colorado Avalanche

Pepsi Center: 1000 Chopper Circle, Denver
Tickets: 303-4AVS-NHL (428-7645)
nhl.com/avalanche

Here's an Avalanche that Colorado loves. Colorado's professional ice hockey team has earned the adoration, too. The Avs, as the team is called for short, won the Stanley Cup in 1996 in their first season in Denver, making them the first National Hockey League team to ever win the title right after relocating. The successes continued; the Avs made it to the Stanley Cup Finals again in 2001 and won again, making the team the only active team in the NHL to ever win all of the Stanley Cup Finals they have appeared in. Add to that 10 division titles, including 9 in a row (the longest streak in NHL history), and it's no wonder these games are popular to go watch and a hot activity for Denver visitors. The Avalanche are part of the Central Division of the league's Western Conference and play in the Pepsi Center.

2 Colorado Mammoth

Pepsi Center: 1000 Chopper Circle, Denver
Tickets: 303-405-1101
coloradomammoth.com

You can't be a sports fan in Colorado without knowing the Mammoth. Although lacrosse is not as big as football is, Colorado rallies behind its box lacrosse team, which has led the league in attendance for multiple years. In fact, one year, the team had greater attendance than Colorado's pro ice hockey and even pro basketball teams. The fan base is warranted: the Mammoth rank pretty high in the National Lacrosse League and made the playoffs every year but one since moving to Colorado in 2003. You can see the team play at the Pepsi Center in downtown Denver. Interesting fact: The Mammoth have the same owner as the Avalanche, Nuggets, and Rapids.

3 Colorado Rapids

Dick's Sporting Goods Park: 6000 Victory Way, Commerce City
Tickets: 303-825-GOAL (4625)
coloradorapids.com

Soccer fans, you must add a Rapids game to your day-trip itinerary. The Colorado Rapids are Colorado's professional soccer club. The Rapids have been competing in Major League Soccer since 1996, as one of the founding clubs of the league. While the team has had some ups and downs, they did win the MLS Cup in 2010. They also competed in the Cup in 1997 but lost to D.C. United. Watch the Rapids players do their thing at Dick's Sporting Goods Park in Commerce City, a soccer stadium built for the Rapids about 10 miles northeast of Denver. The stadium, which also hosts rugby and lacrosse games, concerts, and music festivals, seats 18,000 and opened in 2007. Before that, the Rapids played at Mile High Stadium and then its replacement, Invesco Field at Mile High (now called Empower Field at Mile High).

4 Colorado Rockies

Coors Field: 2001 Blake St., Denver
Tickets: 303-ROCKIES (762-5437)
mlb.com/rockies

Colorado's professional baseball team is the Denver-based Colorado Rockies. The team competes as part of Major League Baseball's National League West division at Coors Field, right in the heart of lower downtown Denver. The stadium is within walking distance of many of Denver's great bars, restaurants, hotels, and attractions, so during a home game, the streets are often flooded with excited fans wearing purple and waving flags. Coors Field opened in 1995 just two blocks from Union Station, a historic train station that is still operating. If you are downtown during a game, you can't miss it. Because the field is so easy to access, tourists can walk right over from their hotel and then hit up a restaurant or bar after the game.

5 Denver Broncos

Empower Field at Mile High: 1701 Bryant St., Denver
Tickets: 720-258-3333
denverbroncos.com

If you know football, you know the Denver Broncos. Colorado's professional football team has an impressive record, including three Super Bowl wins (as of 2019). You can see them play (and probably win, since their record at home since 1970, when they joined the NFL, is the second best in the league) at Empower Field at Mile High (the locals just call it Mile High). The stadium is one of the most famous sports venues in the world; while watching the team, you can also see the mountains to the west and the Denver skyline to the east. In addition to three world championships, the Broncos have played in the Super Bowl eight times and boast 10 American Football Conference championship game appearances, 15 AFC West Division titles, and 29 all-time winning seasons.

6 Denver Nuggets

Pepsi Center: 1000 Chopper Circle, Denver
Tickets: 303-287-DUNK (3865)
nba.com/nuggets

If you like basketball, head to the Pepsi Center and watch the Denver Nuggets take the court. The Nuggets are Colorado's pro basketball team. They began playing in 1967 as the Rockets and were later renamed for Colorado's gold rush history. The Nuggets, a member of the NBA Western Conference Northwest Division, have had some strong years—they finished second in the Western Conference in the 2019–20 season—but are always fun to watch, regardless of their record. Their home base, the Pepsi Center, is a large indoor arena that also holds various other sports games (the Colorado Avalanche and Colorado Mammoth play there), as well as concerts and events. It hosts more than 250 events every year. It's located right in Denver and is easy to access when you want to go see a game. The center boasts more than 19,000 seats for basketball games.

Pepsi Center, home of the Colorado Avalanche, Colorado Mammoth, and Denver Nuggets

Index

60 Hikes Within 60 Miles: Denver and Boulder

Mindy Sink, Kim Lipker

ISBN: 978-1-63404-285-7 • $22.95 • 6 x 9, paperback
288 pages, full color • maps and photos • 3rd Edition

The Best Way to Experience Denver and Boulder Is by Hiking

A perfect blend of popular trails and hidden gems, the selected trails in this book transport you to scenic overlooks, wildlife hot spots, and historical settings. Each hike description features key at-a-glance information, so you can quickly learn about each trail. Detailed directions, GPS-based trail maps, and elevation profiles ensure that you know where you are and where you're going. This guidebook provides plenty of options for adventure—including trails near Fort Collins and Rocky Mountain National Park.

About the Author

Photo: Shannon McTighe

AIMEE HECKEL decided to become a writer at age 5. Today, she has nearly two decades of experience as a professional journalist. Travel writing is her specialty. She is a writer and editor for TravelBoulder.com and a regular travel contributor for *USA Today* 10Best, Fodor's travel books, SpaTravelGal.com, and Tripsavvy.

She has traveled the world to write in-depth series about humanitarian issues in Africa and Haiti, as well as arts and culture in Iceland, China, Peru, and Aruba. She attended college in Germany and is fluent in German.

Aimee wrote a fitness column and an award-winning fashion column at the *Boulder Daily Camera* in Colorado and was a long-time blogger for HuffPost Weird. She was also known as Digital First Media's "Modern Lois Lane" for her work in digital journalism.

Aimee has been the editor of multiple women's magazines and edited/contributed to more than 40 books, including award-winners. She's earned more than 35 national and state writing awards, including being named the top journalism graduate in the nation and one of the top 10 book editors in Colorado. But the greatest honor is being able to make a living doing what she loves: exploring and writing about it.